Dedication

To my family—my husband Bill.
Our children, Lesley, Claire and Wayne.
Our grandchildren, Christine, Lauren and Julie;
Jason and Christopher; Ivy, Pete and Elizabeth;
our great-granddaughter, Cameron.

Contents

Foreword

If you have a parent over sixty-five, she is being joined every day by more than 5,000 people. In the next forty years, elders will more than double, with the fastest growing segment of our population over age eighty-five. By 2030, people over eighty-five will triple to eight million.[1]

It is no secret that people are living longer, mainly due to better care and nutrition and research into diseases of the aging. The "older generation" is classified into three groups: the young-old from age sixty to seventy-five; the middle-old from age seventy-five to eighty-five; and the old-old who live past eighty-five. The Census Bureau predicts there will be at least one million American centenarians by the year 2050.

An interesting aspect is that the young-old and even the middle-old are often coping with the care of the old-old.

Old people are like young people—they vary in size, mental and physical abilities, emotional needs, drive and desire for approval. There are no average over-sixty-fives or over-eighty-fives any more than there are average twenty-year-olds or forty-year-olds.

The caregiver to the elderly person is most often a woman in her middle years. She may be widowed or divorced, needing to work, and perhaps suffering from physical infirmities herself. Sometimes she is also caring for grandchildren while a daughter or son works. The rising divorce rate has increased the need for effective grandparenting at a time when a grandparent is facing not only transitional periods in her own life but also in that of her parents. In other situations, younger couples have the care of a parent as well as children at home or in college.

Horace B. Deets, Executive Director of the American Association of Retired Persons (AARP), says we all have a stake in the concerns of caregivers. "The caregivers, wrestling with the constraints of time and money, are themselves constantly reminded that they, too, may need care some day."[2]

Under stresses unknown thirty years ago, families are well aware of their responsibilities. Help comes from many sources: agencies on aging, adult day-care centers staffed by community and church professionals, social workers, home health care workers, books and television specials, hospice programs.

The Administration on Aging has launched a campaign called Eldercare: the Challenge of the '90s. According to Joyce T. Berry, Ph.D., former U.S. Commissioner on Aging, we need to bring about a national change in attitude before we can plan for our own needs or meet those of our frail neighbors.[3]

Facts, agencies, and research can help in the care of our

parents, but we are not statistics in God's eyes. We are precious to Him and He longs to help us, to guide us in responsible decisions. Even more, our Lord goes through these valleys with us and desires to remove the resentment, guilt, and unforgiveness that beset us. We have access to His wisdom if we ask (Jas. 1:5). And how we need wisdom in making decisions.

Becoming dependent on others for the most basic care is troubling for people of any age, but here we are primarily concerned with the increasing numbers of elderly who need supportive care.

As Christians we begin to ask ourselves, how much is too much? What does it mean to honor our parents? How do I deal with emotions such as guilt and unforgiveness? How we answer these questions is crucial to our well-being and that of our parents.

As middle-aged children we may feel that there are not enough pieces of ourselves to go around to satisfy the needs of a spouse, children, grandchildren, parents, and often an outside job. We may react angrily if we have no time for our own interests or indeed for our own basic care.

As I have seen the growing numbers of people involved in parent care and talked with scores of caregivers, I have wanted to share my experience as an only child of parents who lived first in their own home, then in our home, in their own apartment, and finally in a nursing home. I learned that change is shock and can be lessened by acting at the right time.

Sometimes a parent is taken into an adult child's home at the wrong time. That parent may be too young or still well enough to live alone with some help, or too sick, requiring so much care that an immediate move to a nursing home is required.

I share with you how our gracious God met each need as it arose in our family's life, how I learned to deal with guilt and resentment, how I made decisions at the time of each one's death.

Many other people have shared their experiences and decisions with me and I am grateful to them for that. Several in the health care field have offered their skills and observations. Although this is a personal story, it is Everyone's Story as we move from generation to generation. "For the Lord is good and his love endures forever; his faithfulness continues through all generations" (Ps. 100:5 NIV).

A wise doctor once shared this thought with me and it is one to guide you through each phase of parent care: "You can provide for your parent's comfort, but not for her happiness." These words contain truth, even biblical truth. Happiness and contentment of Christians of any age is dependent upon their relationship with Jesus Christ.

"Hear my prayer, O Lord, and give ear to my cry; hold not Your peace at my tears! For I am Your passing guest, a temporary resident, as all my fathers were. O look away from me and spare me, that I may recover cheerfulness and encouraging strength and know gladness before I go and am no more!" (Ps. 39:12,13 TAB).

1

...

Let Me Know, Lord

"Lord, make me to know my end, and what is the extent of my days, let me know how transient I am" (Ps. 39:4 NAS).

Some old people die suddenly, but for most there comes some change, accident, or illness that interrupts the serenity of their lives and propels them into dependence. Often one little episode alters the course of life.

At eighty-two and eighty-nine, my mother and father were independent. Dad still planted large gardens of vegetables and flowers. His fruit trees yielded their crops under his professional hands. Mother canned and made jam, worked needlepoint, and vacuumed her house. Dad did the grocery shopping and all of the driving. Almost every Sunday they were in church. A doctor who knew them well saw them regularly, prescribing and counseling according to their needs. Theirs was the kind of life most people in their eighties would like.

Suddenly that one little episode occurred.

Mother climbed up on a chair to adjust the hands of her red kitchen clock, lost her balance, fell, and broke an arm. Dad called me, shaken and upset, and urged me to fly to their home in Utica, N.Y., to help.

That particular trip required many decisions. Going then meant leaving my husband, a teenage son, a daughter-in-law and baby who were living with us, and a part-time job. Since there was no other feasible answer, I flew to Utica. Two weeks later, I called my husband Bill back home in Lynchburg, VA.

"Do you think we could manage if I brought Mother and Dad back with me? Her arm is in a sling and she's helpless."

"Where would we put them—with the kids here and the baby?" Bill questioned. Then he suggested, "I suppose they could use our room—we could sleep on the den sofa bed."

It was settled. I flew to Lynchburg with Mother but since Dad adamantly refused to "get his feet off the ground," Bill drove the 600 miles north to bring him back by car.

How Mother enjoyed her trip! Even with her injured arm, she approached her first flight in a spirit of gaiety and adventure. "I've always wanted to fly!" she affirmed happily.

Four months passed before they returned to their home in Utica, ending a period with four generations living under one small roof, each representing different schedules, attitudes, and dispositions.

The Lord did some refining work on Bill and me, molding and shaping us as we asked for His guidance.

SUGGESTING A MOVE

Soon after their return home to Utica, we suggested that they consider moving into an apartment near us in Lynchburg, but they didn't heed our advice. I wrote and phoned them, outlining the advantages. Relatives called me long distance to protest: "We can't take care of your parents—we're too old ourselves. It's up to you to do something."

Bill and I prayed every day that God would show my parents the right thing to do. After six months Mother called to tell us they had put their house on the market. Six months from the day of that call, the house sold. I made several plane trips to try to sort, sell, discard, and pack. I say *try* because neither Dad nor Mother wanted to discard a thing—not a nail or necklace, chair or carton, rug or rag.

The house and basement were crammed with precious possessions and dusty antiques, as well as worthless accumulations. My parents seemed unable (or unwilling) to distinguish between them; they opposed any suggestions.

For several years my aunts and I had encouraged my parents to clean out. Magnificent treasures of our colonial past mingled with stacks of egg cartons and bent nails; heavily varnished old chests lined the basement walls and were crammed with jars, linens, papers, and tools. Towering armoires displayed shelves of florist ribbons, business records, and vases—all from the years when Dad's floral business, E.T. Hermant and Son, was thriving. Valuable tools mixed with dried-up paint cans. Mountains of magazines lined the garage and outbuilding, producing a fire hazard.

"He keeps everything!" my mother snorted, shaking her head at my father.

"Ha, ha, ha!" Dad emphasized his retaliation loudly.

"*Me*? How about those bolts of material you bought in 1950? I never saw you make dresses out of 'em."

"Material, huh!" Mother's nose went up in the air. "Let's discuss what you plan to do with 18,000 clay pots."

"I plan," Dad replied deliberately, "to *use* them!"

SENTIMENT VERSUS REALITY

It was only one of hundreds of heated exchanges that grew louder and more frequent through the years. Somehow they needed these arguments to infuse life into their relationship.

Mother's best pretense at cleaning out occurred whenever we visited them in Utica. Cornering me in her bedroom, she steered me toward one of her dressers and suggested, "Let's look at these things and you tell me what to do with them."

The first time this occurred I was eager and pleased as we carried each drawer, groaning under its weight, and placed it in the middle of the bed. Several hours later, we carried each drawer back just as full, cartons and wastebaskets still yawning at our feet.

While staying with Mother at her home following a hospitalization, we tried again. "What's the use?" I asked angrily. "You're never going to throw out or give anything away."

Mother was angry too. "You have no sentiment. You don't care how important these things are to me."

THE BEGINNINGS OF GUILT

It was the beginning of a long-term battle over the next few years. Frustrated and guilty, I realized that even though I was a grandmother myself, I still wanted my mother's approval; I did not want to hurt or disappoint her. The first real naggings of guilt began to appear—guilt that Jesus would one day remove.

At Christmas time Mother phoned, begging me to come up as she "just couldn't deal with anything." My husband refused to let me fly to Utica during the holidays, saying I must not leave him, our children, and grandchildren. Nor did I want to. This was one of the many times I recognized self-centered attitudes, so often a result of the aging process.

Meanwhile, I had searched for the right apartment in Lynchburg, one that would accommodate my parents' furniture and mode of living. The one I selected seemed perfect. It was on the first floor, but the balcony faced the yard on a second-floor level. I sent them photos of the complex, as well as a floor plan. The rooms were spacious, and it was only a five-minute drive from our house.

For the next year and a half, Mother and Dad adjusted to their new place, making friends with residents of other apartments, getting their own meals, and watching television together. It was good for me to have them close, knowing I would be quickly available in the event of an emergency.

GETTING THE NEWS

That emergency came on a Father's Day. I was about to leave to pick them up for dinner when I received a phone call from Mother. Her voice was pitched higher and louder than usual. "Dad has fallen—and he can't get up!"

"I'll be right there," I assured Mother. Though the drive took only minutes, my shoulders tensed painfully as I sped past houses and trees. During that short mile and a half, I thanked God for His presence and His care. How blessed we are not to know the future, I have thought many times since that day. Hundreds of trips—to emergency rooms, to the hospital, to the nursing home—were yet to come. I did not know that, of course.

"Why Father's Day?" I asked aloud. I remembered

another Father's Day many years earlier when my husband, still shaking, opened the kitchen door to tell me and our three small children, "I've run over our new puppy."

Amid sobs and tears, Bill hurriedly carried the limp body to bury it in the backyard. I recalled with wonder how our oldest daughter, just eleven, quieted us with the words, "We must stop crying! Think how hard this is for Daddy on Father's Day."

Jolted back to the present, I ran up steps and used my key to open the apartment door. I rushed to the bedroom where Dad lay on the floor. He had slipped while bending over to pick up a pencil. Now he lay on his back, totally helpless and in pain.

Because Mother had been asleep in her lounge on the balcony with the door closed, she had not heard Dad's cries for help for at least a half hour. Even with her hearing aid, Mother's deafness caused many communication difficulties. "I waited till I heard her slide open the door," he groaned. "And then I called as loud as I could."

DEALING WITH EMERGENCY

Now Mother was depending on me to do something. I knelt beside Dad and questioned him while covering him with a blanket. Taking his hand, I prayed aloud, which caused Mother to leave the room in tears. To my surprise, Dad also prayed aloud and in great faith. "Help me, Lord. You are my Redeemer. I pray you'll help me now."

Other than offering a blessing on Thanksgiving, I had never heard my father pray aloud in all his ninety-one years. Helplessness was foreign to this man of sturdy German and French parents. Usually independent, Dad could repair clocks, cook a scrumptious breakfast, and give himself daily insulin injections.

At that moment of emergency, I did not ask myself if

this independence had ended, for my father had extraordinary recuperative power and was seldom ill, except for the chronic condition of diabetes. He was careful about his diet, counting and recording calories in a little black book he kept on the kitchen table. He exercised his arms and legs for minor arthritis, kept records of his finances, and wrote his own checks. His lifelong volatile temper had not improved; I seldom spoke to him if he was at his desk, for his bookkeeping had become an increasingly difficult chore, and he hated interruption.

It didn't take long to decide who to call for help.

At that time our son was an emergency medical technician. A young father, compassionate and capable, he arrived quickly and examined Dad. Hearing a roar of pain, he looked up frowning. "His hip is definitely broken."

Two days passed before the hip could be repaired. While Dad was in the operating room, Mother, age eighty-four, sat stiffly, patting his hospital bed. I stood by the window, watching birds dip their wings as they avoided a protruding hospital column. Suddenly I smelled antiseptic and heard the door of Dad's room open wide. Wearing rumpled green, Dr. Miller whisked off his cap and smiled at Mother and me.

"Some break!" he exclaimed. "In four places. We've put in pins." Shaking his head, he marveled, "Ninety-one years old with muscle like a man of forty. Amazing."

Dad was indeed an amazing man. Though born in the days of the one-room schoolhouse (I still have the slate he used), and with only a ninth-grade education, he had an engineering mind, inventive and discerning. His humorous poetry expressed a grasp of the world's future problems long before the words *additives* and *pollution* were everyday language. Part of a lengthy poem he composed in 1935 reads:

17

In these days of indigestion
It is oftentimes a question
As to what to eat and what to leave alone.
For each microbe and bacillus
Has a different way to kill us
And in time they always claim us for their own.
There are germs of every kind
In every food that you can find
In the market or upon the bill of fare.
Drinking water's just as risky
As the so-called deadly whiskey,
And it's often a mistake to breathe the air.

As a lifelong florist, (a vocation thrust upon him by family pressure), my father did more than grow, plant, and sell flowers. He climbed ladders and stairs, coaled boilers, repaired trucks, chopped wood, hammered, and hauled. No wonder his muscles were strong!

DEALING WITH DAD

That night after surgery, however, Dad's strength became a deterrent to rest—both his and mine. Dad's age and diabetes limited the choice of medication; delusion, hallucination, violence, and terror were his bedmates.

Weeping, I tried to control him as he tore at the tubes in his sutures.

"Please," he whined, "get this contraption off my leg!" His blue eyes penetrated as he accused me of harassing him. "How can a daughter treat her father this way?"

I called for the nurse, who informed me that he could not have a sedative; however, she could hire an aide to relieve me for the rest of the night. Gratefully, I accepted. Returning home at 2 A.M., I sank exhausted into bed.

DEALING WITH DENIAL

Because of my father's extraordinary health and vitality, I refused to believe that grit and physical therapy would not restore him to independence again, regardless of age.

As I left the hospital one day, I met a minister friend at the front door. The perfume of blooming bushes, the penetrating warmth of a June sun, and my natural optimism lifted my spirit—until my friend asked about Dad.

"He's doing great. Cleans everything on his hospital tray. And they took him to therapy again today."

"What will you do next?" Bob asked. "Have you looked at nursing homes?" For a moment I couldn't answer. "Why I expect he'll do well enough to get back to his cane and go home," I said.

Bob was silent as he looked at me carefully for a moment before he spoke.

"He'll never be up and around again. Not at his age. This takes too much out of 'em." Bob turned on his heel and waved. "See you later."

He ambled across the street as I stood there with weak knees and a tightening in my chest. The perfume and sun were gone. In my heart I knew he was right. I had watched Dad in therapy as he perspired, his arthritic hands gripping the bars, his face contorted in pain. I knew another move was coming. And I knew that a change meant shock.

PREPARING FOR THE NEXT MOVE

I prayed what I call my "prepare prayer." So often I have asked God to prepare the way, prepare the heart, prepare me. Two definitions of *prepare* are to "make ready" and to "make receptive." As I turned to the Lord for the next step, I asked Him to do just that—to prepare

19

the place, and to prepare the hearts of Dad and Mother—to accept the next move.

In looking for the right nursing home for a parent, choices can be limited, as mine were, by availability. If the needs of a parent are primarily for skilled care, investigate this type of provision.

Perhaps, however, a parent cannot be kept at home for reasons other than physical incapacitation. In that case, facilities for companionship and recreation, as well as nursing care, are of paramount concern. Finances usually are a major factor. Dad's immediate needs were for nursing care and physical therapy, and I considered the proximity of the center, too, for my convenience.

When Dad was moved by ambulance to his new space—half a room—I thought of his background. He had lived most of his life in the same area, witnessed the moving of New York's Mohawk River and the installation of the Barge Canal. He had delivered flowers by horse and buggy, sometimes driving through ice and water. His spacious property housed tractors and tools, barns, trucks, and greenhouses.

Now he had two drawers, some clothes and slippers, a few books, and a razor. How we need to know that for most of us life shrinks; only our relationship with Christ expands, *if we choose Him early in life.*

The reality of birth, life, and death pressed in on me as I settled my father in his room, soothing, answering him, and loving him. I did love this lusty, loud, and sometimes irritable old man. I had been born when he was forty-two, his only child. He had wanted a boy, but I never felt I was supposed to be a boy, nor did my father reject me. In fact, late in life, over and over he told me, "What would we do without our daughter!"

Life was never the same again after the day he bent over to pick up a pencil and fell.

This once-robust man plodded forward with a walker, painfully . . . haltingly. . . . The body and mind that had functioned smoothly, even brilliantly, gradually deteriorated, expressing signs of helplessness and senility.

"And now my soul is poured out within me; days of affliction have seized me" (Job 30:16 NAS).

I, his only child, watched, prayed, and learned; meanwhile, caring also for a mother whose strength gradually failed.

ANOTHER MOVE

Soon after Dad entered the nursing home, the doctor advised us that Mother could not manage alone in her apartment, which confirmed my observation. She frequently had dizzy spells when she got out of bed at night to go to the bathroom or when she turned too quickly. Suppose, alone in her apartment, she fell and lay there for hours? I thought of how long Dad had lain helpless before Mother heard his cries.

Sometimes food burned and the kitchen exuded smoke while Mom napped in her bedroom. At these times Dad's keen sense of smell had rescued them. But now who would check on Mother?

"I'll never come to live with my daughter," I heard my mother say when she was younger. But life has a way of changing those decisions for us. With the expense of Dad in the nursing home, we could not stretch the income to meet costs of an apartment and round-the-clock help (even if available). Once again my husband and son moved the furniture, this time into our basement.

TIME TO CONSIDER

1. When you must make a decision quickly, what influences you most? Prayer? Friends and relatives? Think of the past: How has God equipped you for this moment of decision? Trust that He will lead you now.

2. Do you feel prepared to handle crises or emergencies? Although Jesus admonishes us not to worry about tomorrow (Matt. 6:34), we do need to think through possibilities as our parents age. Think of ways to improve your communication with them and siblings.

3. The author says change is shock. If you need to move your parent(s) to your home or a nursing home, how can you minimize their shock? How would you prepare other members of the family?

4. Read and meditate on Philippians 4:4-10.

2

...

The Things of Others

"Look not every man on his own things, but every man also on the things of others" (Phil. 2:4 KJV).

Charles was rubbing Dad's scalp with a flourish one day as Mother and I arrived at Dad's room. He did it with an air of professionalism, whisking the towel into the air and capping the bottle of antiseptic noisily. "This is very good for dandruff," he affirmed.

Mother had not yet noticed what he was doing. Holding on to the foot of the bed, she eased herself into the chair. Failing eyesight and hearing, as well as lack of concentration, usually combined to make her oblivious to her surroundings. Dealing with this aspect of old age was very difficult for me.

"Well, how are you, Daddy?" Mother asked her husband.

Compassionate Care

While they chatted, Dad in his wheelchair, and Mother leaning forward to hear him better, I turned to Charles. He was a tall, thin man about forty, one of the certified nursing assistants in the nursing home.

Six men were his charges, and he was responsible for all their personal care. This included baths, making beds, cleaning up after accidents, giving enemas, and supervising meals. Charles had a gift for his job—a desire to please and a natural ability to communicate with elderly men. He knew when to baby them and when to be stern. Giving the scalp treatment was an example of his "going the second mile" for those in his care.

Smiling, I said, "Charles, I really appreciate your care of Dad. There aren't many like you."

He raised his eyebrows just a bit, indicating his thanks. "Well, the Listerine is almost gone. You might want to buy a bottle. It's cheaper than if they buy it for you."

"All right." I glanced down at his feet. "Say, it looks to me like your ankle is swollen."

"I twisted it, and it sure is sore. Well, I must see if Mr. Elton has finished his lunch." In a limp and a flash he was gone.

Imagine my astonishment when I learned the next week that Charles had been fired.

"He's an alcoholic," the nurse told me, "and it's such a shame."

"A shame!" I cried out." "He's the best worker here. He has taken such good care of Dad, and Dad really likes him. Couldn't you keep him anyway?"

She shook her head. "It's been going on a long time. He doesn't show up some days—doesn't even call. We can't depend on him. He was given three warnings. Then yesterday he came into work drunk."

SHOWING INTEREST IN THE STAFF

When a parent becomes a resident of a nursing facility, family members relinquish some responsibility. To ensure proper care of a loved one, however, it is necessary to know the staff. The apostle Paul instructs, "Look not . . . on [your] own things, but every man also on the things of others" (Phil. 2:4 KJV)—the interests and concerns of others. In this case we must not only bear the burdens of caring for parents' needs, but of understanding the problems of the staff who serve our loved ones.

Eileen, a middle-aged CNA (certified nursing assistant) who had been on staff for three years, went home after a seven A.M. to three P.M. work shift to nurse her own mother. Joe, another orderly, went to school full time and worked the eight-hour night shift. Alice was a capable charge nurse whose husband was dying of cancer and whose son lay unconscious after a fall at a construction site.

As I visited my father day after day, week after week, bringing my mother with me, I felt compassion for these people who worked under difficult personal circumstances. How often I heard visitors complain, expecting far more of these "servants" than they themselves would be willing to give.

Showing interest in these workers builds a rapport which often results in an opportunity to share Christ. Encouraging them to give the best of themselves to their jobs and offering words of appreciation at the right time is beneficial to them and to those they care for.

Though I no longer worked as a broadcaster and writer at a local radio and television station, I continued to write from home. A Christian magazine published my four-generation household story, and Dad had a copy at his bedside. One by one the CNA's and nurses read the article, which resulted in several opportunities to share the joy of the Lord. A few confided their current heartaches and asked for prayer.

Dorothy, a CNA in her mid-thirties, suffered from anemia. She was tiny, too, and I often wondered how she lifted some of the patients. One day, noticing her ashen face and eyes dark with fatigue, I asked her if she felt all right. She replied that she did not and that she was waiting for results of her latest blood test.

She was a Christian and had shared with me her mother-in-law's recent death and brief glimpse of heaven's beauty as she died. Dorothy had been with her. "I loved her very much," she told me. "She was only fifty-two, but I know where she is."

Dorothy's kindness spilled over in the care of her patients. I watched her gentleness as she coaxed one old lady to eat her lunch, calling her "Sugar" and encouraging her, patiently spooning food into her mouth.

Then one day I saw Dorothy in the lobby, painfully propped in a chair waiting for her ride home. She had helped prevent an old man from falling to the floor, and as the patient resisted her, she had injured her own back severely. She was never able to return to work.

DEALING WITH THE DIFFICULT

Not all the nursing assistants are kind and loving; not all make good decisions, nor do all know how to treat their charges.

I am thinking of John, whose every move and gesture signaled rebellion in his job. A student at a Christian college, he worked part time and evidently hated every minute of it. Many aides simply take the job because it's a way to earn money. For a few weeks John was Dad's orderly, snapping the sheets as he made the bed, angrily pushing the wheelchair. He rarely spoke to Mother. One day all his resentment burst forth.

"Come to the shower room with me," he demanded. "I can't do anything to please him!"

Dad's disposition was less than pleasant, and at this time, and in this place, and at his age, it had not improved. However, I had grown used to him, knowing what should or should not be said. John had neither the time nor the inclination to try.

I followed John as he pushed Dad's wheelchair to the men's shower room. Breathlessly I ran to keep up. Settled on the shower chair, naked and shivering, Dad fussed and winced in pain. John indicated the faucets and the temperature gauge. "He complains it's either too hot or it's too cold. Watch." John was shouting above the rush of the water.

"OOOOh, that's cold!" yelled Dad, as if on cue. As John changed the flow, Dad hollered that it was too hot. I let the water run on my wrist. It felt pleasantly warm.

"John, I think it's okay. Look, you have a temperature gauge, why don't you go by that and the feel of it yourself? Just do the best job you can."

"Well, he hauled off and hit me one day," John said, gritting his teeth.

I had no doubt that Dad had. As Dad progressed—or regressed—into senility, his physical strength increased, and sometimes he fought wildly—hitting, kicking, yelling. The worst was ahead, but I left John to complete his job of showering my father.

I was not surprised one day to find that John was no longer there.

The importance of caring helpers is illustrated in a letter we received from Elsie, the daughter-in-law of Bill's Aunt Kate. Aunt Kate (Nana) had finally adjusted to her surroundings at age ninety-five and Elsie wrote:

27

Nana stays about the same and doesn't complain anymore—in fact she tells us how nice everyone is to her and that the food is good.

Now our troubles have started with my mom and dad. As you know, Dad has had two strokes and is becoming more and more of a care. He is very demanding and is now up about every two hours all night long. He is pretty good in the daytime—watching television and smoking his cigars. He eats beautifully and never complains, but the evenings and nights are becoming worse and worse.

Mother was taken to the hospital suddenly about a month ago because of bleeding. They took all kinds of tests and finally removed a polyp from her stomach. They did this down through the throat so there was no surgery required; however, she is very weak and run down. The doctor finally said she could no longer take care of Dad.

I had to stay with him around the clock for about a week and a half and then I was able to get two sisters to stay with him on a 24-hour basis for $100 a day. They were in their forties and had to alternate every two days because he called for one thing or another so often. I think the week and a half that I stayed with him took ten years off my life. I don't know how my mother stood it as long as she did.

Anyway, Dad is now in a private rest home. He is really getting more care than in the place where Nana is and that is supposed to be the best in the area. I don't know how long they will keep Dad because it is not a health-related or a skilled nursing home, but they have very kind, caring aides who are taking care of him beautifully. It's so much more like home than the bigger places.

Mother stayed with me for about a week when she came home from the hospital and then I had her out for dinner every night for another week. Now she is home and just needs to get her strength back. I hope she doesn't insist on keeping that big house because it's just too much work for her, and Bob cannot take care of two places.

Martha's situation was stressful too. Her mother was kept at home in a lovely apartment but required round-the-clock aid. This meant that Martha was responsible for finding, interviewing, hiring, and firing any number of nurses, sitters, or aides. The interpersonal difficulties were enormous. Not only did we pray for nurses for Martha, but we asked God to give her discernment about the problems between her mother and the helpers. Sometimes helpers are jealous of one another; sometimes it is difficult to know whether the aide is really incompetent or if the patient is imagining things which are not true. Such situations are not only trying, they cause anger and stress in both parent and adult child.

BEARING ONE ANOTHER'S BURDENS

To look upon the interests of others—to bear one another's burdens—the Bible is clear on these points (Gal. 6:2). One day at the nursing home, Paul, a friend whose mother-in-law was also a patient, discovered a thoughtless change made in the living habits of a blind patient. She had been moved to another room, and since she was in the bed near the window instead of the one near the door, she was unable to move about in her darkness without stumbling.

Paul found her one day groping for a familiar night table which, because of the reverse furniture arrangement,

29

was located now on the other side of the bed. This patient had no family; a bank conducted her affairs. Paul advised the charge nurse that little Miss Whiting should be returned, if not to the same room, at least to the familiar side of the room, where she could feel her way around in confidence.

The administration obliged and Miss Whiting again became oriented to the familiar surroundings. In addition, Paul took the time to hold her hand and pray with her and explain what had happened. Before that, little Miss Whiting, bank account or no, had no one to be her advocate.

SUGGESTIONS FOR VISITORS

If we are regular visitors to nursing homes, we need to pray that we may be the helpers God desires—knowing when to become involved and to what extent.

In order to bring balance and common sense into our visits with a parent or friend in a nursing home, we need to be alert to specific ways of sharing, listening, and just being there that relieve the distress and anxiety experienced by those in the home and those who visit.

Not all of the following suggestions apply to every resident; each is in a different state of health and possesses varying abilities of comprehension and enjoyment. In addition, it is good to check with the charge nurses before bringing food, flowers, or other items that might be inappropriate for health reasons.

• **Share food.** Most residents eat meals alone. Bring two glasses and a milk shake; divide a favorite dessert; cut a piece of fruit and eat it with a loved one. Eating *with* the person lets him know that we enjoy his company and encourages eating. Sometimes a treat left on a bedside table is unnoticed or forgotten if nursing assistants do not help the person eat it later.

Occasionally, order a hospital tray and share a full meal together. This is a way to learn firsthand the quality of the food served, and an opportunity to observe the ability of the person to feed himself, as well as to enjoy fellowship.

• **Share reading material.** Perhaps a parent can no longer hold reading materials or see well enough to read. We can read a passage from Scripture, or from the church newsletter or daily newspaper. If we sense the person's mind has wandered, we can repeat the reading. Often attention spans are brief. Touching may help reinforce awareness as we read.

We can recall past activities together, even if they weren't ours, by bringing an illustrated magazine that expresses a parent's former hobbies or interests.

Sometimes correspondence addressed to the patient is left on the table or in a drawer and may be unopened. We can read it aloud slowly. If the parent is able to write, encourage signing seasonal greeting cards to friends and relatives. We can address the envelopes.

• **Share beauty.** Bring one lovely flower in a vase and tell where it came from—garden, a friend, or a florist shop. When bringing or sending a greeting card, choose one with bright colors and bold print. Gold lettering and pastels do not impress dim eyes. Colored snapshots of children, grandchildren, and pets; calendars with bright scenes; small crafts—all express love and cheer. Better yet, bring grandchildren or great-grandchildren in person. Most nursing homes allow children to visit. Outgoing youngsters will climb on laps with smiles and hugs; shy ones learn about caring through such visits.

Sharing beauty may also be a pleasant pastime in the warmer months if the patient can go outdoors with help or in a wheelchair. Small things we take for granted often please aged people: the rustle of leaves, the songs of birds, visitors and employees coming and going through the front door. My father admired the different models of cars pulling up to the door, while Mother scrutinized the changing fashions and hairdos. Involvement wards off apathy and depression.

When programs and performers are brought to the home for the residents' enjoyment, try to attend occasionally. Recreational activities have a lot to do with the mental health of the patient who is able to share, watch, or participate. Complimenting the director of recreation, offering to assist occasionally, particularly at holiday functions, and attending once in a while, combine to encourage programs at these facilities. We should also encourage the parent to attend or participate if he is able.

• **Stay awhile.** This is not always convenient, especially when we have other family members at home to care for, or a full-time job outside the home. Usually it is more important to visit less often and stay longer, unless the loved one is extremely ill and it is necessary to visit daily to encourage the patient.

Sitting by the chair or bedside is an opportunity to catch up on some of our neglected chores, such as reading business reports or opening mail, writing a letter, or making a grocery list. Watching TV together is another possibility if there's a set in the room.

When a parent has been hospitalized for a long time, constant personal attention is not necessary. Our relaxed presence, even though we are doing something, relates our caring. Sometimes such a period of quiet encourages the person to share thoughts, fears, or questions that he or she might not otherwise bring up during a brief stay.

• **Listen.** This can be discouraging, especially when parents or friends can no longer communicate meaningfully. Minds wander, they hallucinate, and recall incorrectly. It is important to keep our own minds and hearts on Jesus during these difficult times. We can't dismiss a parent's anxiety with simple cheer; rather we must take complaints seriously and check with those in charge. Ask the Lord for His wisdom and guidance. A parent's peace of mind often depends on reassurance.

RELATIONSHIPS IN BALANCE

The Christian life is one of relationships. Balance is needed as we learn to express ourselves to others, to listen with our hearts as well as our ears, and to take the actions we understand to be right. There is a tension between our actions and our obedience to God's Word and His will. He is gracious to hear us and to instruct us as we tune in.

TIME TO CONSIDER

1. What are your reactions to the words "nursing home"? What are your parents' reactions? Do you know anyone who works in one?

2. If your parent is not in a nursing home, have you visited one recently? Plan to do so and talk with the administrator. Ask about the ratio of nursing assistants to residents, including the night hours. Ask for a tour.

3. What is the difference between the phrases "bear one another's burdens" and "each one shall bear his own load" (Gal. 6:2, 5)? How do they complement each other? How do they relate to the relationship between you and your parents?

4. In reading the suggestions for visiting in a nursing home, would you add any others? Do you disagree with any of the author's ideas on visiting? Why or why not?

5. What does it mean to listen to others with our hearts as well as our ears. How can we "tune in" to hear God?

3
...

Not As We See

"For God sees not as man sees, for man looks at the outward appearance, but the Lord looks at the heart" (1 Sam. 16:7 NAS).

"Well, the Lord knows my heart."

Have you heard people say that to cover up a tactless remark or questionable action? Perhaps you have said it. I have, and in a self-righteous manner that I know grieved my Lord. We think that we can excuse ourselves because we believe that deep inside we have a right motive. We think we know our hearts, but in Jeremiah we read, "The heart is more deceitful than all else and is desperately sick; Who can understand it? I, the Lord, search the heart, I test the mind" (17:9-10 NAS).

In all of us (even in those with so-called low self-esteem) there exists a level of ego that says what I feel inside is what is important. There is, however, a sphere of thought and motive that is known only to the Lord. We need to ask Him if that sphere is pleasing to Him.

Considering relationships with our parents will be more fruitful if we first assess our relationship with God. We must ask, "Is Jesus Christ Lord of my life?" When we want God's will above ours in every situation, we have made Him Lord. *Want* is the key, for then God can show us, can guide us through His Word, through circumstances, and friends, through quiet communion with Him. During the mid-years of our lives, no greater blessing is ours than to know the Savior in such a way. Then we can share Him with our aged parents, and can teach our children and grandchildren the serenity that comes from Him. "The weak need My strength. The strong need My tenderness. The tempted and fallen need My salvation. The righteous need My pity for sinners. The lonely need a Friend. The fighters need a Leader."[1]

Let us pray, "Lord, show me now where I really am in my relationship with You. Help me to be truthful to You and to myself. I desire to please You and to be free from guilt, resentment, depression, and fear. I know and affirm that these do not belong in my life if I am to serve You and others."

WHERE ARE YOU?

_____ I believe in God and I pray now and then.

_____ I believe in God and go to church, but I don't have a personal relationship with Jesus.

_____ I believe in God and know Jesus died for my sins but I am too busy and tired to think about it or to pray.

_____ I accepted Jesus as my Savior when I was young, but I seem to be living my life alone now and trusting in my own strength and abilities.

_____ I read the Bible, but it doesn't have real meaning in my   life.

_____ I was raised in a Christian home and apply these principles to my life. I try hard.

_____ I have too much resentment and guilt in my life to think that God would ever forgive me or care about me.

_____ I am so angry with God for all the trials and tragedies in my life that I can't pray or read the Bible.

_____ I am a Spirit-filled Christian and I have peace about my relationship to the Lord.

_____ (Fill in the way you feel).

No matter which appraisal or appraisals you checked, there is hope. Jesus came to give abundant life (John 10:10) and He is able. You may begin a new life with Him right now, receiving forgiveness and the gift of the Holy Spirit. God knows what is in your heart, but He wants you to acknowledge your feelings to Him. Tell Him you are willing to unburden yourself and cast your cares on Him.

We need to spend time with Him as we do with a loved one to know He forgives: to know that trials come to us for a purpose (Rom. 8:28). As we deal with crises and trials, having a flexible personality carries us through. Being so in tune with God as to perceive His timing in situations is learned and comes from spending time with Him. While we jog, drive to work, vacuum, take a shower, or wait in a doctor's office, we can effectively meditate on a verse and ask for His wisdom. His Word is stored in our hearts, to be released in times of need. There is no substitute for this, whether we are saints of many years or new Christians.

CARING FOR MOTHER

For a year and a half Mother lived with us while Dad was in the nursing home. This meant that three times a week I drove Mother to see Dad. Preparing for the visit took a great deal of time, for Mother moved slowly. Bathing, dressing, eating—all took longer. As I tried to clean house, wash, and prepare meals, she would call frequently. The faucet wouldn't work, her earring dropped, her pocketbook disappeared.

One snowy day as we returned from our visit with Dad, my small car stubbornly wedged its wheels in the snow at the end of our long winding driveway. Had I been alone, I could have abandoned it there and walked to the house, but Mother couldn't walk. I called Bill at work and he arrived in twenty minutes, but was unable to move the car. Mother, shivering, began to chuckle. She thought it an adventure! Imagine her delight when her ingenious son-in-law assisted her into a metal lawn chair, and pushed her, sleigh-fashion, up the long driveway to the door! During the next few years, Mother forgot the names of her grandchildren, whether or not the doctor had visited, and what she had for lunch, but she never forgot her winter adventure!

Soon after this winterlude, Mother failed rapidly. Her cataracts had progressed to the point where every room was too dark or too light for her. She needed regular assistance in the bathroom and with bathing. Dinner time was a struggle. What should have been a pleasant time (Mother loved to eat) became a tense time. Unwilling to adjust to our schedule, she insisted on hers. Though we got up at 6 o'clock, Mother slept till 9 (when she expected a substantial breakfast). She liked to listen to nightly television till 11:30, with the volume so loud we couldn't sleep. When we requested that she turn it off, she became angry and pouted. During this time her physical needs increased and in lifting and helping her I injured my back.

The woman now struggling to navigate a walker had

once danced around the kitchen while dinner cooked. Her voice, now slurred and sometimes raspy, had yodeled like an Alpine climber and sung hymns in harmony. Hands that once could knit and crochet couldn't button a sweater.

MISSING THE BEST

Something was gone—a *joie de vivre*, an energy that was exclusively hers. I was her only crutch, a link with the past. Somehow at this period we missed the best in one another; we were not free enough to be fully honest. Though we shared in prayer and she asked me questions about the Bible, though in earlier days we went together to Christian Women's Club and Women's Aglow meetings, somehow the difference of generations was markedly present in our relationship. Our interests were totally different. The most sewing I did was to replace a button or suffer through a hem, while Mother executed Swedish darning and intricate needlepoint. The most reading she did was an occasional magazine, while in earlier years I read every book in our bookcase. Mother put off letter writing indefinitely; I wrote stories from the age of seven.

I know now that Mother's demands for attention were a replacement for occupations of the past; my neurotic attention to those demands was my way of renewing a childhood obedience, no longer appropriate for a woman in her 50s.

What really caused me great concern was the effect all of this had on my husband. He had been hospitalized a number of times for heart and pulmonary problems, and I observed the strain of Mother's demands on him. One morning, after a particularly difficult day for all of us, including a visit to see Dad, I "took my prayer station." Sitting on a sofa that faced a large window, I opened my Bible and read, "I will stand on my guard post and station myself on the rampart; and I will keep watch to see what He will speak to me, and how I may reply when I am reproved" (Hab. 2:1 NAS).

I needed reproving. I felt angry with my mother, trapped by her demands. Bill and I had so little time to talk or share alone; and if Mother turned on her television, it was so loud, our conversation competed with the screeching wheels of a TV show. Asking her to close the door offended her. Yes, I felt trapped between pleasing a mother as a little girl should and being the wife God intended me to be.

As I sat before Him that morning, I asked Him to help me, to show me His answer. Once an energetic, well-balanced woman, I had become shaky and irritated. "Father, forgive me," I prayed. "I am afraid for Bill. I acknowledge before You that I fear for his health. I want wholeness for all of us."

God knew my heart. He knew I had thought about Mother being with Dad in the same nursing home. She needed help now; I had no time for anything but her care. Of course the Lord knew my heart. When friends said, "Oh, it's so hard for you—your mother with you and your father to visit too!" I felt fleshly self-pity rising like a fresh batch of dough. They saw the outward appearance, but the Lord saw self-pity, resentment, anger, rebellion. There was nothing to hide from Him that day as I sat before Him.

SEEKING AN ANSWER

Then peace began to flow through my body. I seemed to hear the question, "Who is first? Your husband or your mother?" I dialogued with God: "Lord, I really want Mother in the room with Dad. Then I could visit them together, and Mother would be with her husband, and I with mine.

40

I thank You that they have money, and I trust You to give me the right answer. Free me from self-pity, fill me with Your Spirit and Your wisdom."

I sat a little longer. No sound came from Mother's room. Then I prayed in a way I had not prayed before. I "put out a fleece" (Judg. 6:36-40). I knew this wasn't a good way to pray on a regular basis, but I felt led to do this. "Father," I whispered, "if this is Your will, let there be a room available when I call the nursing home." At 9 o'clock I phoned and talked to the administrator. No, there wasn't a room available. As I hung up, I was disappointed, yet I knew from the peace in my heart that God was faithful. I could trust Him. Mother was not yet awake—I usually had to call her several times while preparing her breakfast. As I set a place for her at the table, the phone rang. It was 9:15.

"Mrs. Fanning?" It was the administrator at the home. "I was mistaken. The man in the room with your father has just been checked out, and the bed in his room is available for your mother."

My prayer had been answered, even to the exact room; but I had yet to face Mother with this new arrangement!

EXECUTING THE ANSWER

A big red pickup parked in our driveway. Two of our friends loaded Mother's recliner and television into the back. Inside the house, I packed a suitcase with flannel nighties, two velour robes and slippers, some underwear and dresses, a pair of sturdy shoes. Deodorant, powder, hand lotion and pill bottles fit into a corner.

"My pocketbook," Mother said urgently. "Be sure I have my pocketbook." I handed it to her. An old blue leather, her favorite, it was filled with white hairpins, loose pennies, and a hanky with lace edges, along with an old red wallet, bulging with snapshots, and containing a few dollars. She owned two new wallets, Christmas gifts from past years, but they always remained packaged and the familiar went with her. A giant print Bible, a calendar of Florida scenes, and her glasses case also were packed.

The car door open, I waited, helping her settle into the front seat. Jim and Les had already pulled away in the truck. I was glad. I didn't want to follow it on the expressway, our eyes fixed on those two pieces of furniture tied to the panels.

As I think back to that day, I am filled with wonder. In a matter of hours, I had talked with Mother, called our friends who had the truck, packed her belongings, and settled Mother in the room with Dad! With the decision made, all things fell into place as we made this drastic change in our lives.

That morning after breakfast I had helped Mother to her chair where she tried to read the paper, at least the headlines. I prayed as I approached her, knelt by her chair, and told her of my decision. "I just can't handle it any more, Mom," I said to her, my insides rubbery.

To my surprise, Mother looked straight at me. "You're tired," she nodded. "It's all right, Budsy" (a favorite nickname from childhood).

How God puts it all together for us when we truly seek His will and guidance. He knows the end from the beginning. That very day He knew that in a few brief months our daughter and her two small boys would be seeking shelter in our home.

Actually, some aspects of that day are not too clear in my memory. Mother's admittance to the nursing home, the unpacking and conferring with the staff, my encounter with an angry doctor I should have consulted first—all blend with the pleasant surprise on my father's face when he realized his wife of fifty-two years had come to share his space! "Now we can watch TV together in this motel!" he exclaimed. Dad's understanding of his accommodations ranged from being in a travelers' inn to a place where there were "inmates." His mind had begun to unravel, and during the next year I would be picking up the threads.

By now you may be asking, "How could you do that? I would feel so guilty! What did your husband say?"

At 5 o'clock I was back home preparing dinner when Bill walked in the door, threw his briefcase on the counter, and strode to the bedroom to change clothes. "Hi!" he hollered en route to his destination. Bill, six-foot-three, is not slow; every move is purposeful.

"Hi!" I called. In a few minutes Bill was back in the kitchen, a puzzled look on his face. "Where's Mother?"

"In the nursing home with Dad," I answered. Then I shared the events of the day. A man not easily rattled, Bill was flabbergasted. "You *what*?"

By the look on my husband's face I knew God's will had been accomplished. I may not recall all the details of the day, but I do remember the relief and surprise on his face, a relaxation of wrinkles, a clearness of eye that I had not seen for a long time.

To be honest and scriptural, I must admit I should have discussed this with my husband first, even though it was my mother and not his. But this was an unusual day. I know it was right because never once did I regret the decision I made the day I sat before God and put out a fleece.

CONSIDERING PRIORITIES

Personally I feel that where a spouse is involved, we must prayerfully consider the situation of priority. Sometimes, of course, there is no other solution, particularly in a tight financial crunch; but those of us with spouses who suffer health problems must remember we could sacrifice their health, and even lives, under certain conditions.

This reminds me of Gladys, whom I met at a Christian writers' conference. After the conference, she waited with me at the gate at O'Hare airport, since her plane did not leave for another hour. Her pale violet eyes and delicate skin were framed by softly curling white hair. Gladys' sweet spirit mixed with a gentle sadness had attracted me the first time we discussed our interests. Gladys wrote Sunday School leaflets for children. As a widow, she lived alone, surrounded by her daughter's family and dependent elderly relatives. "My mother lived with us from the time we were married," she offered softly. A little shocked to find out that her mother was only fifty-four at that time, I inquired about their relationship.

"Mother's hearing was extremely poor," she said. "And my husband said, 'Gladys, your mother will always have a home with us.'"

"You had a daughter. Did that cause any problems?"

"Not really. Of course, Mother was always there to do things around the house, so Susan didn't learn much about housekeeping."

"Did that bother you? I mean, did you feel your mother took over your place in the house?"

Gladys' voice was soft, slow. "Sometimes I did, but Mother was real good, easy to live with. And we had so many relatives living near us who needed help—my husband's and mine."

I moved closer to Gladys to avoid being jostled by travelers going everywhere and nowhere. Setting my briefcase on the floor and shading my eyes from a sudden burst of sunlight, I pressed on. "Did you and your husband ever feel a lack of privacy?"

It was harder now for Gladys to talk. She seemed to be listening to something. The noise of departing planes, the voices on the intercom, the crying of babies: none of these were sounds she heard. The sounds came from the past, perhaps. "At first it was all right," she said. "Mother was sensitive to our need to be alone, but as she grew older, she wouldn't leave us alone. I had to be very firm and insist, and then she would pout."

"That was hard for you, wasn't it?" There was something here I needed to know and my plane was boarding!

"Yes, oh, yes. And now Mother's in a nursing home, and she was so glad I could come to this conference. But those other years. . . ." A rim of tears formed circles around the violet eyes. Then they splashed forth, finding little wrinkled crevices in which to lie.

"Those years," I said quickly. "What years?" I picked up my briefcase, boarding pass ready.

"My husband has been dead for five years now." The softness was still in her eyes as she said, "Oh, how I wish I had spent more time with him and less with Mother!"

I embraced Gladys one last time, sorry that I had uncovered her pain, but knowing it was therapeutic for her and helpful to me to share with others. Up the ramp I hurried, thinking I might never see this dear lady again.

Gladys told me her husband reminded her that anything they did for others was done for Jesus. "Inasmuch as you did it to one of the least of these My brethren, you did it unto Me" (Matt. 25:40). Doing the will of God in honoring our parents and caring for them requires a balance. There is also the injunction concerning marital status: to leave parents to be joined to a spouse (Eph. 5:31). And if single, a life of service to Him may not include care of a parent. It may be a matter of priorities.

SORTING TRUE GUILT FROM FALSE

If you are in a similar crisis, you may be confused, haunted, or disturbed by different factors. Perhaps you promised a parent that you would never put him or her in a nursing home. Phrased that way, it indicates abandonment—and abandonment of a parent *should* cause guilt. Effectively dealing with the trauma of care by entering a parent into the best facility you can locate should not cause guilt, provided you follow through with your responsibilities. Honoring a parent includes a willingness to love, share, listen to, and respect that person, no matter what his state of health or dependency. Honoring means praying for your parent. It does not mean being a doormat, dealing with the parent's demands to the exclusion of others' needs, or your own. If under duress you made such a promise, and you feel duty bound, I suggest you first pray alone, then counsel with your pastor or other mature Christian, preferably someone who has been in the same situation and reacted in a stable manner. Discuss it with your spouse.

Often, married men whose parents are living with them, leave most of the work and parent-relating to wives, and this can cause serious marital difficulty. A husband's mother is his responsibility, and his wife will appreciate his interest and concern in the personal aspects, not just the financial and practical.

One great-grandmother of my acquaintance, who died at 102, defiantly dared her son to "put her away." For ten years this strong-willed lady harassed her son in his own home, almost drove her daughter-in-law to a breakdown, and browbeat every aide they hired to help with her care. One evening we saw this woman and her son and daughter-in-law in a restaurant. This tiny lady of ninety pounds

46

yanked her son away from us as he tried to converse. She behaved like a spoiled child of three, but the son allowed her to treat him this way. It was only after her 100th birthday, bedridden and mentally unstable, that she entered a nursing home.

SHOWING COMPASSION

In this era of child abuse, we also hear about physical abuse of parents. It is more common (even among Christians) to relate to a parent in a way that is emotionally abusive, perhaps without even knowing it. To replace that kind of abuse with compassion is vital.

Compassion makes us see beauty in the midst of misery, hope in the center of pain. It makes us discover flowers between barbed wire and a soft spot in a frozen field. Compassion makes us notice the balding head and decaying teeth, feel the weakening handgrip and the wrinkling skin, and sense the fading memories and slipping thoughts, not as a proof of the absurdity of life, but as a gentle reminder that "a grain of wheat remains a solitary grain unless it falls into the ground and dies; but if it dies, it bears a rich harvest."[2]

No one answer is right for everyone when parent care decisions are made. All the factors of life must be included: health of family members, stability of the marriage relationship, effects on children living at home, finances, God's will at the time. The latter can be assessed only through a relationship with God, a life yielded to Him. Whether a parent is kept in his own home, our home, or a nursing home, compassion and caring are factors under our control with the help of the Holy Spirit, for He provides strength when we believe our endurance has reached its end.

In their book *When Your Parents Grow Old*, Jan Otten and Florence Shelley write:

> Your parent may react very strongly to a move from one place or kind of residence to another. Uprooting can be a psychological shock, creating new health problems or intensifying existing ones. But no solution will be perfect if your parent is ill and old and tired. Whatever you do, in or out of his home or yours, if it is done in love and compassion, with respect for your parent, for yourself, and others in your family, it will be the best you can do. This is all anyone can ask of himself.[3]

Now is the time, wherever we are in life, to affirm a right relationship with God—not when we are up against difficult decisions and strained endurance, or have reached old age. Praise is a vehicle we can use to affirm this now. Kathryn Parker Knudson, a grandmother, expressed it this way:

> I have awakened. It is early. No one is stirring. My whole soul turns to God in worship and adoration. My body, oh, it is miserable, dull; it feels stupid; it says it wants more sleep. My heart and mind are heavy. Living death ever haunts one's way, springing out at every turn, and in every quiet hour. But from all of these I was delivered long ago, the night I crossed the Red Sea, and so my soul is free to worship the One I love.
>
> Welcome, sunshine, rain, snow, or howling storm—it does not matter. It is God's day. Welcome,

joy or sorrow; welcome, sickness or health, abundance or lack, friend or foe, companionship or solitude, strength or weakness—what does it matter? My Heavenly Father orders my days--what comes or goes, all has been committed to Him. I have just one care, and that is that I rest in Him. I want to live this day for His glory—and how can He be glorified in me if I fuss and complain and grumble and sigh and moan and lament?

I am Thine, O beloved Lord, and Thou mine, and unto Thee I give thanks for everything. Thou hast put a song in my heart, and that is what the world shall hear from me today.

When we know the Lord in this way, we shall be content, wherever we live.

TIME TO CONSIDER

1. Think about the sentences you have checked on the list "Where are You"? Are you honest about your assessment? Do you fall into more than one category?

2. List differences in interests, attitudes, and approaches to life between you and your parent. How do these affect your present relationship? Do you see any way to effect positive changes?

3. Do you try to "hide" from God? Read Matthew 15:18 and Mark 7: 20-23. Can you identify any sins of yours not on the list in Mark 7? Ask the Lord to reveal them to you.

4. If you have to place one or both parents in a nursing facility, what would be your biggest emotional struggle? Guilt? Fear? Can you define "true" and "false" guilt as they relate to your parent?

5. Do you agree with the author's definition of "honoring a parent"? Why or why not?

4

...

She Has Done What She Could

"She has done what she could: she has anointed My body beforehand for the burial" (Mark 14:8 NAS).

One of my favorite accounts in the Gospels is the one about Mary's anointing of Jesus with costly perfume. It was six days before the Passover, and the disciples had gathered in Bethany at the home of Simon the leper. Whether it was "an unnamed woman" or Mary, the sister of Martha and Lazarus, who did the anointing, the account is the same in Mark and John, even to the kind of perfume. The perfume was nard, a very expensive fragrance imported from India. How Mary obtained this, when it was worth as much as a day laborer earned in a year, we do not know.

Consider the scene. As was the custom, Jesus and the disciples were lounging at the table, which was most likely filled with fine figs and pomegranates. The smell of delicately prepared fish probably whet their appetites, yet it was a tense time. The chief priests and Pharisees had given orders that if anyone knew where Jesus was they should report it. As Jesus rested at the table, Mary approached Him, her loosened hair falling over her shoulders. She took the beautiful flask from her robe, quickly broke the seal, and began to pour the liquid over Jesus' head. No doubt those who watched gasped, but by this time Mary had tearfully and passionately poured the last drops over His feet. Then she wiped His feet with her hair, while tears mingled with the perfume. So powerful was the sweet aroma, that the smell of food had lost its pungency. By then the disciples were aware of the fact that her act of devotion had cost 300 denari. Judas was not the only indignant disciple. Would not most men have considered this a waste? Jesus had always emphasized caring for the poor. But now He announced that her deed would be remembered whenever the Good News is preached. Jesus declared "she did what she could."

This is a comforting, freeing, and satisfying statement when we apply it to the care of aged parents. Mary could have wrung her hands, followed Jesus everywhere, worried about His future, His every need. She could have brought Him a plate of fruit, a specially prepared cake, and that would have indicated her caring. Perhaps she could have offered to wash His robe in the river, or run errands for His disciples. But in one loving, dramatic moment she said it all: "I love you, Lord. I know, as well as You, what is ahead. Let me anoint You, my King, with my most precious possession."

Certainly, had she sold the perfume, many widows and orphans would have had a feast; perhaps lepers would have worn new robes; poor women with no cooking utensils would have had some vessels for their meager meals. Jesus knew that, but He also knew Mary's heart. She had put her life on the altar; she did not care if she was reported to the Pharisees.

SHARING CHRIST'S LOVE

I am not advocating that we carelessly throw away money or possessions when they should be given to the poor, or that we become irrational givers without proper thought to stewardship. Those of us inclined to fret, worry, and fuss over our parents, doing small things to assuage feelings of guilt, need to learn that nothing we do for them is as important as sharing the love of Christ—our most precious possession—with them. If our parents are the ones who taught us of Christ's love, they need to see the fruit of their teaching in our lives as we minister to them; however, many Christians have parents who do not know the Lord as Savior. The leading of the Spirit is important as we minister Jesus' love and the Good News. Indeed, these are the only realities we can give them as life drains away. Once we grasp the truth of doing what we can, ministering to our parents becomes less emotionally wearing. Some parents' demands are so excessive that children who frantically respond to them become ill physically, emotionally, or both. Then they are no help to the aged person who needs *them* most. It sometimes hurts to say no to a parent, a friend, or a child, but often it provides balance and wholeness for both parties. On the other hand, some parents demand so little, protesting that they are burdens, that adult children aren't sure when they are properly helping their loved ones. Both situations cause tension that needs to be faced and understood.

DEALING WITH EMOTIONS

Forgetfulness and confusion of parents can result in unhealthy responses. I routinely visited my mother three times a week, so I was totally unprepared for the storm one afternoon when I entered her room and approached the bed where she was resting. Angrily she attacked me. "Where have you been? You haven't been here for a week!" Since she had appeared cheerfully responsive two days earlier, I was deeply hurt. My father, far more confused, would often say, "I haven't seen you for three months!" But I could always kid around with Dad and bring him back to reality. Mother's attack on this particular day (which occurred some time after my father's death) startled me into anger and tears. I ran out of the room, down two flights of stairs, and sat in the lobby. I felt so depressed, so unappreciated, so weary, that I almost left for home.

What did it matter, I thought, since she didn't know how often I came, if I came at all? I shut my eyes and said *Jesus*. Calmness flowed through my body, removing anger and hurt. After several minutes of prayer, I returned to the room. I asked the nursing assistant to get Mother up in her chair. Neither of us discussed the incident, though I could see she remembered it. "I was here Tuesday," I defensively told her. But what did that matter? Tuesday, Thursday, Friday—they were all alike to her amid a tiresome routine. It's important to try to inject change into their days.

"Let's go outside," I suggested a few moments later. "There's a lovely breeze."

There is no substitute for God's healing of emotions when such deeply hurtful incidents occur. Forgiveness of one another is necessary, but it's sort of like applying ointment on a bruised knee: external ointment soothes temporarily, while complete healing is slower and is accomplished only by the God-given healing properties of the body. So it is with our emotions.

Whether it be guilt that comes from recognizing our sin that needs to be healed by God, or only a neurotic response to our parent's words or actions (that may require counseling), depression, physical ailments, and loss of energy often result from these encounters. Not only do we feel the negative results in ourselves, we show it in irritability and anger toward our families and even toward the staff at the medical facility where a parent is cared for.

Most staff persons at a good nursing home are trained to help the families of new patients as they seek to make this transition. Kay Newman, an R.N. whose love is geriatrics, was a charge nurse while my parents were patients. "It's very hard on families," she told me. "Some of them suffer guilt from the realization that they neglected their parents in earlier years and are suddenly faced with a very helpless parent who needs nursing home care. It's not unusual for the person to indict staff members for problems that are not our fault. For instance, one lady felt we had abused her mother because she suffered bone fractures. The real cause was osteoporosis. We were really extremely careful when we moved or turned her."

Kay's love for old people was reflected in her advice and admonition toward the nursing assistants. "I tell them to give the kind of care they would like for their own parent."

MISDIRECTING OUR EMOTIONS

We need to recognize that guilt can cause us to do too much or too little for a parent, or it can cause us to misdirect our emotions toward others. If we are suffering from guilt in our parental relationships, it is time to look at our priorities and other responsibilities, including our jobs, spouses, children, friends, and churches. When guilt becomes so excessive that it intrudes on other aspects of our lives, we must establish priorities. Some find it helpful to write down priority and time-management lists. Each of us is unique in our energy levels and our need for rest. Our biological time clocks must be adjusted to the added responsibility of being caregivers to parents. If parents expect too much, we must say, "I cannot do that."

URGENT OR IMPORTANT

In her book *How Do You Find the Time?* Pat King, mother of ten writes: "Every time the urgent is put first, the important takes second place!"[1] Many items on the agenda of an elderly person appear urgent. We need not take care of what appears urgent in order to feel we are performing properly. Instead, having established our own priorities, we do the important. Then the urgent falls into its proper place or often disappears.

During the eight years that my parents required help and supportive care, life did not stand still for Bill and me, and it will not for you. Our years spewed forth such traumas as my major surgery, Bill's many hospitalizations for heart and pulmonary problems, the death of our daughter Claire's first two babies, the birth of our daughter Lesley's premature baby who spent almost two years in a body cast, the birth of a baby girl to our son and his wife while they were both still in high school. A few years later, Claire and her two little boys came to live with us temporarily; her husband's drinking, gambling, and abuse eventually flung their marriage into divorce.

Friends and acquaintances dealt with such heartaches as children who were into drugs, in prison, or suicidal; others suffered crippling illnesses, widowhood, or loss of jobs while they coped with the life endings of parents who had once sustained them. God is indeed faithful. When we truly know Him, He gives us joy and turns our mourning into dancing! Nothing is too hard for God; His arm is not shortened! We need to establish communion with God through Jesus Christ His Son as early in life as we can.

During a sermon entitled, "Our Comforting God," our pastor, Dr. Lowell B. Sykes, said:

Life has a way of falling apart. We get one situation straightened out and something else comes up to plague us. Again, the aggravation is illustrated in the old cartoon of the Three Stooges in which they are trying and trying to get the top drawer of a dresser closed. They struggle with it and finally it bangs shut. But as it does, the bottom drawer pops out and hits them in the shins! That's the way life is. Sometimes we can laugh at it, but many times we cannot and we sob with frustration, "Lord, how long can I stand this? One thing after another!"[2]

Later in the same sermon, he said:

The things that perhaps you wish most had never been a part of your life—had never happened to you—as they are given to God, can be the very bridges over which you can bring compassion and comfort into another's life. If you had never known that failure, if you had never experienced that sin, if you had not been close to that particular death, if that depression had not settled on you like a black cloud, if you had not been through the anguish of that physical pain, you would never have any idea what a person is going through who had experienced those things."[3]

57

Compassionate Care

We do what we can with what we have. When Jesus is first in our lives, we know we are forgiven and can forgive others. When we learn to cope with the many difficult situations in our lives, we can indeed affirm Paul's expression: "Blessed be the God and Father of our Lord Jesus Christ, the Father of mercies and God of all comfort, who comforts us in all our tribulation that we may be able to comfort those who are in any trouble by the comfort with which we ourselves are comforted by God" (2 Cor. 1:3).

TIME TO CONSIDER

1. Are you able to say no to a demanding parent? Why or why not?

2. If your parent needs but refuses help, in what ways can you help?

3. How can Jesus' words, "She has done what she could," help you with your responsibilities and priorities?

4. Are you able to separate the important from the urgent in parent care? In other family relationships? In your job? Why or why not? (If not, you might want to talk to a pastor or counselor).

5. After reading this chapter, how would you pray for yourself? Write out your prayer, asking the Holy Spirit's help.

5
...

Being Worthy

"He who loves father or mother more than Me is not worthy of Me. And he who loves son or daughter more than Me is not worthy of Me" (Matt. 10:37).

One of the most frequently asked questions by adult children concerning aging parents goes like this: "My eighty-two-year-old mother's driving skills have deteriorated drastically and I'm worried that she may have an accident. When I hint that she should give up driving, she gets angry. What can I do?"

This is a common and serious problem when adult children are caring for their parents. Serious, because based on the relatively fewer miles they tend to travel, the elderly over age seventy-five have a modestly higher accident rate than most other driver groups, according to a National Research Council study done specifically to address transportation in an aging society.[1]

Just as teenagers often drive too fast, elderly people frequently drive too slowly. Both endanger other motorists and pedestrians. Owning and driving a car are the last activities elderly persons wish to relinquish, yet they react differently. Some assess their own situations and decide to drive only for short distances and not at night. Others are angry and defensive or give up in resentment and expect instant auto service from friends and relatives.

My father drove his Cadillac from New York to Virginia till he was in his late eighties. He was a good driver with excellent vision. During one trip, the car was hit broadside by a motorist who ran a stop sign. Mother and Dad managed to drive their damaged vehicle ninety miles back to Utica, buy a new one, turn around the next day, and continue their trip! Understandably, when they sold their home and moved to Virginia, Dad (at ninety) was unwilling to sell his car and quit driving but the shock of moving and his advanced age caused a rapid deterioration in his driving ability. When I suggested he make this change, he balked. Then one day during a routine medical checkup, I spoke privately to the doctor about my concern. In our case, the doctor proved to be the successful intermediary.

As we drove home, Dad remarked, "The doctor says my arm is too lame to continue driving. He called it taxi driver's arm. I told him I had driven trucks for years. I guess it's better if I give up driving."

Instead of telling Dad he was too old, slow, or inefficient, the doctor gave him an acceptable reason. Later, when Dad's arthritic arm hurt, he remembered that. "Good thing I stopped driving," he would say.

Perhaps your parent would be willing to curtail her driving rather than stop altogether. Could she drive only short distances and not at dusk or at night? Should her medicine be checked for compatibility with driving? Has her vision and hearing been evaluated recently? If you do not live near her, find out if her community offers transportation services for seniors.

FINANCIAL DECISIONS

Other areas of concern to me were Dad's management of his finances and the possibility of his suddenly becoming incapacitated. Mother was not authorized to co-sign checks or other documents. For years she had asked him to simplify his investments. Mother always did the bookkeeping for the business, but Dad alone managed the money and made all financial decisions. After talking to a lawyer, I asked my father if he would be willing to give me power of attorney, promising that I would not exercise it unless truly necessary. He had always trusted me, and in this case, having no brothers or sisters simplified matters; but Dad was adamant—the answer was *no*.

It is usually necessary for the one writing the checks, paying the bills, and sorting the insurance and Medicare claims to have power of attorney. In cases where there are many brothers and sisters, a meeting or telephone conference call may be needed—perhaps with an attorney present. When my father finally agreed (not happily) to give me this legal right, we signed the papers and I promptly put them away. One day they would be needed quickly. Till then, I allowed Dad to struggle along doing his own finances.

A cousin in her sixties discovered that her father, who lived alone and suffered from dementing illness, was stashing his Social Security checks under the mattress and hiding hundreds of dollars in the kitchen cupboards and refrigerator. Finally, against his will, he was moved to a private home, whose caregivers understood him and provided him with a homelike atmosphere and good country cooking.

ROLE REVERSAL

Role reversal may be an overworked term, but how do we say it better? Once these fathers helped us with math, gave us allowances, and said no when we wanted to use the family car. Mothers made us brush our teeth and change our dirty clothes. Now *we*, their children, make these decisions for *them*.

Sometimes a parent makes the obvious solution difficult. In thinking through the problem, I realized that my love for my parents, my sense of duty, my desire to ease the responsibilities they had formerly borne, only served to cement them more firmly to the walls of their past. Their generation of Christians, so rooted in the law and ethics of the Old Testament, had struggled frugally and faithfully executed duties foreign to many young people today. To have a daughter insist on change of any kind provoked them to anger, and even despair.

FEAR OF DISAPPROVAL

Mother's attachment to her family—even her ancestors—was so deeply rooted that she couldn't part with possessions that various family members had owned. Some articles were indeed valuable; others were plainly rubble. Even after moving twice, our garage looked as though we were storing materials and furniture for an entire community. Bill and I decided to sell some of the furniture that remained and add the income to the estate. My own reluctance to deal with such matters showed me I still suffered from fear of disapproval, a characteristic probably more common to only children.

As our parents age, and as we age, there needs to be a

tension accommodation, a sincere effort to see the other person's position. Mother's life had revolved around one area of the country and a large family who had settled there. They visited and accumulated, married, buried, and depended on one another as members of a tight-knit community. Though she could not tell me what to do with these possessions, neither could she let go enough to approve of their disposal. It was seemingly an unsolvable matter.

In Psalm 39:6 we read, "Surely every man walks to and fro—like a shadow in a pantomime; surely for futility and emptiness they are in turmoil; each one heaps up riches, not knowing who will gather them" (TAB).

Not having our own houses in order presents others with the difficulty of disposal. There is indeed a balance needed here. We read in I Corinthians, "And those who deal with this world—over-using the enjoyments of this life—let them live as though they were not absorbed by it, and as if they had no dealings with it. For the outward form of this world—the present world order—is passing away" (7:31, TAB).

This last passage is more pertinent today, perhaps, than in any other period of history. World unrest, terrorism, hunger and homelessness, toppling governments, and financial collapse everywhere we look suggest to us that personal possessions be of low priority and that we obey our Lord's command to "occupy till I come" (Luke 19:13 KJV).

SEEKING THE KINGDOM

Mother did not have her mind only on the treasures of earth, however. Some passages of Scripture were puzzling to her, and as she grew older and closer to the Lord she desired answers. One day we had a discussion about the Second Coming, and I read several passages of Scripture to her. She was most puzzled about Jesus' statement, "He who loves father or mother more than Me is not worthy of Me. And he who loves son or daughter more than Me is not worthy of Me" (Matt. 10:37). These words in Luke disturbed her even more: "If any one comes to Me and does not hate his [own] father, and mother [that is, in the sense of indifference to or relative disregard for them in comparison with his attitude toward God] and [likewise] his wife and children and brothers and sisters [yes] and even his own life also, he cannot be My disciple" (14:26, TAB).

From a commentary we also got this help: "The Gospel deepens human love, and often natural affection and loyalty to Jesus are compatible (Luke 18:20; Matt. 15:4-9), but when there is a conflict, the claims of Jesus come first. Jesus' followers, therefore, should not be moved by mere emotion or motivated by easy hopes."[2]

Where those emotions lead and how we view the *idols* of our lives is crucial to our own aging process and the *tension of accommodation* between us and our own children as we age. Jesus said to seek first His kingdom and His righteousness and all these things would be added (Matt. 6:33). I suspect He knew that when the hearts of His followers were first on the kingdom, "all those things" would be fewer and less important.

Life has a way of removing the worldly from us. Houses are torn down to make way for shopping malls, investments fail, possessions burn, are stolen, or delegated to someone else, but Jesus Christ is the same yesterday, today, and forever! (Heb. 13:8).

BEING WORTHY NOW

Our renewal in the Spirit promises power and victory, not only when we eventually join the circle around the throne, but in the here and now. Singing to the Lord and praising Him with prayer and Scripture feeds our spirits as we seek to be worthy of our calling as disciples.

How can we live as though this life will never end—accumulating, idolizing, closing our ears to the call of the Spirit? We do it, impatient, fractious, possessive people that we are, no different from the Israelites throughout biblical history.

If and when we hear God's call and understand His leading, how do we put it first, before our love for parent and child? Wisdom and balance are required as we seek to be worthy of Jesus' call.

When Jesus told the man to follow Him and not take the time to go back and bury his father, I hear Him saying: "If you wait till all your earthly duties are discharged to come and follow Me, the time may not come for you. You'll miss the kingdom. Put Me first, ahead of the demands of parent and child."

We all have places in the body of Christ, exercising our gifts and following our callings. God does not expect us to abandon these callings, though He may change our directions. That is why studying and listening are such vital parts of our faith.

MEETING PARENTS' CHANGING NEEDS

Some aged parents expect Christian children to abandon callings or life-styles in order to accommodate the parents' changing needs. A parent may want to keep a home, to hold on to his holdings and independence, and cannot always see the disruption he causes in his children's lives (including fighting among siblings). We, as these children, need the balance of honoring parents without dropping our own lives, which have been ordered by God, in order to pick up theirs.

For many of us, this is one of the most difficult balancing acts we will face.

To be effective servants in role reversal calls for willingness to

Accept what has happened. Wishing will not push back time. Wasting energy on regret over past decisions, poor choices, or failures is futile. Affirm the time. It is today. Go on from here.

Accept our personhood. We are precious to God. He understands the responsibilities in our lives—our marital status, our jobs, our financial and health requirements. We *do* need rest and change; our parents are not our only responsibility. All that appears urgent is not necessarily important. Time for renewal and rest are vital to being effective servants in the kingdom.

Accept our parents' personhood. Whatever illness of mind or body a parent has suffered, he or she is precious to God. That he can no longer function independently or as well as he did in his earlier years, does not make him any less valuable to God. Praise is as important to growth in old age as it is for children. Small improvements and achieved goals encourage the old as well as the young. Contrary to statistics, some old people are able to learn new skills, revive old interests, and more importantly, accept the Lord Jesus as personal Savior.

Accept counseling. Some of us think because we are Christ's disciples, we don't need help. Our emotions, misunderstandings, and deep-seated hurts sometimes combine to make it difficult or impossible to function properly as caregivers to parents. If this happens, feel free to acknowledge it and seek counsel from a pastor, a professional counselor, a trusted friend, or even an adult child. Expressing pain or getting another's perspective can break the stalemate and move us forward.

The Lord himself is my inheritance, my prize. He is

my food and drink, my highest joy! He guards all that is mine. He sees that I am given pleasant brooks and meadows as my share! What a wonderful inheritance! I will bless the Lord who counsels me; he gives me wisdom in the night. He tells me what to do. I am always thinking of the Lord; and because he is so near, I never need to stumble or to fall. Heart, body, and soul are filled with joy. For you will not leave me among the dead; you will not allow your beloved one to rot in the grave. You have let me experience the joys of life and the exquisite pleasures of your own eternal presence (Ps. 16:5-11 TLB).

TIME TO CONSIDER

1. If your parent refuses to give up an activity or responsibility (such as driving or finances) that she can no longer do adequately, how do you handle it?

2. Do you still need your parent's approval? Why or why not?

3. How does this chapter's scripture (Matt. 10:37) affect you? What conflict might this scripture cause in your life? Is Jesus your first love?

4. How can you "parent your parent" and still be respectful? List your parent's losses in life. Which life changes are hardest for her? In what ways can you help her accept them?

6

...

Strength
for the Weary

"He gives strength to the weary and increases the power of the weak" (Isa. 40:29 NIV).

"Every crisis seems to happen over a weekend or a holiday," sighed my cousin Bev. "My only time for a breather and then—no time."

Bev and her husband Evan, who both held full-time jobs, had cared for his father in their home, and after his death, invited her ailing mother and stepfather to live with them. No longer well enough to manage alone, the older folks occasionally were hospitalized—usually on Bev's day off.

"I used to think we'd be gone before they were," added Evan. "And though our teenage daughter was helpful and respectful, they criticized her every action or opinion. We thought an answer was to have a housekeeper come in every day. But that was even worse. Bev's parents complained and I felt like an outsider in my own home, unable to pad around in my pajamas or express myself freely. The housekeeper didn't please us *or* our parents!"

COMPLICATIONS OF CAREGIVING

Caregiving today is complicated by two factors: more women working and family mobility. The first means less available time (not always bad when the parent is demanding) and the second, long distance caregiving. Job transfers and parent retirement relocations separate families in our generation. In her book, *Who Cares for the Elderly? Public Policy and the Experience of Adult Daughters*, Emily K. Abel writes, "Policy makers who tout the superiority of family care and seek to return care to the home cling to a romantic vision of a world that has ceased to exist. . . . Women responsible for care at home frequently hold waged jobs. It is critical that policy makers base their recommendations on an understanding of the reality of contemporary caregiving rather than on nostalgia for a mythical past." [1]

Many caregivers with outside jobs juggle job performance with worries about the elderly parent left at home. Did Mom take her two-o'clock medication? Is she messing in the kitchen? Has she fallen?

For some caregivers, adult care centers located throughout the country have answered that problem. They serve clients full- or part-time by providing individualized care for frail or disabled elderly whose children work or who need a break from full-time caregiving. Many of these centers, often located in hospitals or churches, are funded by their state's department for aging, since it is less costly in the long run to intervene early. Providing interim respite for caregivers, whether or not they hold outside jobs, these centers also extend the mental and physical abilities of the aging through activities and companionship. Cost is reasonable and financial aid is available.

"We provide respite care in the home too," Gwen Naples, a nurse at an adult care center told me. "Doctors become so focused on the medical needs of the parent, they often don't see a caregiver on the brink of exhaustion. We encourage doctors to hand out a written prescription saying, 'Get help for yourself!'"

When I asked Naples for her "best advice," she said, "Don't wait till it's too late; Don't wait till you're exhausted!" On their own initiative, Naples' parents had moved recently to live close to her in the event they needed help.

When both my parents were living with us, along with our son, his wife and baby, I tried to keep working part-time. Two days a week a helper came in to clean the house and prepare lunch. For a time that worked, but eventually I found it less stressful to stay at home.

"I'd go crazy *without* my job!" says Wanda East, Educational Co-ordinator for Camelot Nursing Home in Lynchburg, Virginia. Like many independent elders living alone, Wanda's mother, eighty-four, is headstrong and self-willed. "Mother manipulates me," says Wanda. "One day she'll say, 'I'll stay in this house till I die!' and the next time she's telling me I won't make any other arrangements for her. Nothing I do pleases her!"

Widowed several years ago, Wanda says her second husband, who is retired, is "an angel to my mother and so patient. Sometimes she calls him to pick her up and when he gets there, she's gone off with someone else!"

As I talk with women who are caring for parents in some way, I hear frustration, anger, guilt, and resentment.

All these emotions make it harder to continue the wearisome chores and contacts necessary to their care. Often their past relationships intrude into every aspect of care. Many of these elders were always angry, controlling people; others were alcoholic or abusive; some are just lonely and become dependent on the adult child for every need.

In her book *Caring for Your Aging Parents*, Barbara Deane tells us to set limits, for it's certainly true we can't please dependent parents all the time—nor should we try.

Deane writes, "To set limits is to assess realistically (1) what your parent needs (not wants); (2) how many of these needs you can meet, taking into account your responsibilities to yourself and other family members; and (3) who besides yourself can meet some of these needs."[2]

A VARIETY OF AVAILABLE SERVICES

If you are reading this book propped up in bed after a hard day of work and wondering what you can do about a parent who lives far away and is failing, I have good news. Today there is a wide variety of services for the aging in every community.

Perhaps your parent or a sibling has been calling you long distance indicating need for evaluation. Beth Ulrich, Director of Social Work for a large hospital complex and a Christian whose own mother lives several hundred miles away, is encouraging about help. "Any hospital social work department in your parent's community is a good place to start," she says. "Hospital social workers usually know what is available there—area offices on aging, personal care agencies or departments of social services. Specialists with the aging also know how to deal with older people's resistance which may be part of your problem."

Ulrich suggests gathering information, then planning a few days off to visit your parent, having made appointments in advance to see key people. Doing research ahead of time saves time while you're there.

The American Association for Retired Persons (AARP) tells us that it is important to make the most of your time when visiting an out-of-town relative by being observant without antagonizing the elder. Is there anything unusual about your parent's eating habits or his or her contact with others? Are finances being handled properly? Are there obvious safety problems?

"*Before* there's a crisis, check in your parent's community for resources," Ulrich advises. "This is especially important if you must work and also live out-of-town. Do your homework before a need arises."

Ulrich suggests meeting with siblings if possible. She admits frustration with people who have never made any plans or thought about the possibilities of change in their parents. Often when the parent is discharged from the hospital, families think he or she can continue life as before. That was my feeling after my father broke his hip. We don't want to admit a major change may be imminent.

Gwen, an editor, says her 91-year-old aunt has been in and out of the hospital-to-nursing facility twice in six months. Even though Gwen and her mother thought her aunt couldn't make it on her own, she pulled herself together and lives in her apartment with a walker, day-time care, and a "Help" button around her neck. "She could fall and break something during the night," says Gwen, "and she needs help with her checkbook, but she's content in her own place. We realize that she's in that in-between stage, so we pray a lot!"

Lois Kasenter, who grew up in the Pennsylvania community where her mother lived all her life, says it's important not to be swayed by others in your parent's community when you're a long distance caregiver. "I felt the pull of the community where I grew up," says Lois, "and I had to search my heart for my mother's needs without regard to the way others viewed me or talked about me."

Lois feels support and counsel from people where you live helps you keep a clear head. Her mother, who was trying to operate the family farm all alone at age ninety, is now reasonably happy in a retirement community near her old home.

Geriatric care or case management is a relatively new field which can help the long-distance caregiver. Members of the National Association of Private Geriatric Care Managers (NAPGCM), these managers help in a crisis, counsel, monitor outside services for your relative, help with medical appointments, transportation, or paying bills. In other words, they do the kinds of things you would do if you lived near your parent. This service is costly, but may be just an interim help for you. Your Area Office on Aging or AARP can give you more information on this service.

GOD'S PROMISES OF STRENGTH

Often parental crises occur at times when our own lives are in distress or pressured over other problems. That's when God's promises of strength and power for our weakness are so precious. Sometimes we need a counselor or friend to help us see this. Shirley (not her real name), a friend who came to me for support, suffered from depression and was being counseled professionally by a mutual friend. She was caught in the "sandwich," trying to cope with children and elderly parents. I've asked her to share her story:

"I've learned you can't 'fix it' no matter how hard you try. I was a perfectionist who needed everything to be right; I am a wife, mother and daughter who thought I could be all things to everybody. Well, I couldn't. First, my husband Don was transferred to another state, actually bringing us a little closer to his parents and mine, who lived a hundred miles apart. That meant leaving lifelong friends in my mid-years and moving two older teenagers who didn't want to come. As a nurse, I worked part-time and I was very lonely. That's when everything broke loose. My mother and Don's father died, both leaving frail spouses. We made trip after trip every weekend, driving over 200 miles each way.

"At the same time, we began to have crucial problems with our children, both of whom are adopted. To me the adoption process had put extra pressure on my perfectionist child-rearing. I needed to prove I was qualified to raise these children. Well, our daughter Stacy became pregnant and I felt out of control. I worked, but I needed to go to our parents' each weekend. I was angry with my pregnant daughter, who released her baby for adoption into a Christian home. Our parents and other relatives never knew about the pregnancy.

"I kept all this to myself, and though Don was wonderful and kind, I sank deeper into depression, trying to "fix" my life. I wanted one large leap to make it all better, but my healing was a gradual process.

LEARNING TO SAY NO

"Through counseling, I learned I could say NO to 'duties' at church and to family members. I've learned I can say NO and still be a caring Christian. I can't 'fix' our parents' old age and I can't live my children's lives. I continue to work and I realize that Don and I have a marriage to preserve and enjoy.

"What has helped me most was having a Christian woman counselor—I believe a woman understands our feelings best—and her 'prescription' of reading the Psalms

and listening to praise music. Oh, how that music minis-
tered to me! When I couldn't concentrate on my church's
prescribed daily Bible study (and felt guilty that I
couldn't)—just the Psalms and the music lifted me from
the pit. I feel free, knowing my Lord is the one in control,
and there is only so much I can do. I can't control other
people's choices and feelings.

"We've met with siblings near our parents and are looking into alternative care for my mother. And now—I'm
taking time off to go on a business trip with Don."

My cousins Bev and Evan say they have no regrets
about caring for their parents. "My mother was always
generous and thoughtful toward me," says Bev. "If I have
any resentment, it's toward my stepfather's children, who
left all the care to us and seldom visited or helped in any
way. We lived through several trying years. After work
and a long commute, I was exhausted and needed time
alone before dinner, but never had it. But now it's over,
and though I still have to work, I look forward to retirement, hoping I can learn from our experience to become
the older person God would have me be."

Many people have received help from a simple exercise
my husband shows audiences or congregations as he speaks.
"Hold out your hands, palms up," he says. "In the left, place
your problems and burdens, your questions and cares. Now
see that the right hand represents God's sovereignty and
power. Place your left hand in your right and say, 'You are
in control, God. I give all of this to you.'" By doing this
visual and verbal action, we sense a peace from God.

"Do not be anxious about anything, but in everything,
by prayer and petition, with thanksgiving, present your
requests to God. And the peace of God, which transcends
all understanding will guard your hearts and your minds in
Christ Jesus" (Phil. 4:6, 7 NIV).

TIME TO CONSIDER

1. If you're working, does that make it harder or less stressful to deal with dependent parents? Why?

2. Is it possible to present your problem to your employer in the event you need time off? (Many employers have been through this themselves.)

3. Reflect on the type of relationship you have had with your parent. How does that fit in with your present situation? Does she WANT help or is she reluctant to receive advice? Can you think of ways to help her face the present from your viewpoint? Read James 1:5 and 3:17.

4. If your parent lives far away and needs help, write down your options. List organizations and people who could advise you. Ask your spouse, siblings, or prayer partner to pray with you about these.

5. Where do you place God, your job, your spouse, your children, your parents, yourself in order of priority? Do you think you can "be all things to all people"? If not, list family members, friends, or agencies who could help.

6. If you are depressed, confused or feel unable to cope, have you considered Christian counseling? Taking time for that may save you time and effort in the long run.

7
...

My Complaint Is Rebellion

"Then Job replied, 'Even today my complaint is rebellion; His hand is heavy despite my groaning. Oh, that I knew where I might find Him, that I might come to His seat!' " (Job 23:1-3 NAS).

"And the people spoke against God and Moses, 'Why have you brought us up out of Egypt to die in this wilderness? For there is no food and no water, and we loathe this miserable food.' " (Num. 21:5 NAS).

I heard quiet laughter coming from my parents' room at the nursing home. Then my son's cheery voice. "It was such fun, Grandma. Baskets and baskets of 'em. Of course I ate more than I brought to the house!"

Grandma leaned closer to hear him better. "You helped

me stir the jam, remember?" she asked.

Grandpa's head lifted. "I'd like some of that jam now, Mother," he said.

She glanced toward him. "Wish I could do it. I'm no good for anything anymore."

Wayne, her grandson, reached for her hand, "Oh, now, Grandma, don't say that. We love you. Just remember I haven't forgotten those good times I had at your house."

Strawberries, of course. That was the topic. Adult grandchildren have a way of lifting spirits through reminiscing that we, as the children, do not. As soon as Mother saw me, she squinted, lowered her chin and grouched about her dinner. "Look! Who could eat *that*?"

I looked at the plate on her tray, its untouched Swiss steak cut into small pieces. I took a bite.

"It's tough!" Mother said. "Tough!"

I didn't think so, but I had all my own teeth. I turned to my son. "Sounds like you and Grandma were having a good time." Wayne gave his grandmother a kiss and announced he was off to work.

One of our daughters lived in the same city and visited too. She and my mother always had a special relationship; some sort of generational chemistry existed between them. "She was a special grandma," Claire told me.

Even in her 70s my mother picked berries with the children, made play spaces for them in the garage, and allowed them to help with cookies. Now it was hard for the grandchildren to watch her feeble attempts at walking, those painfully swollen legs clumping along like inanimate pillars.

Often we hear that grandparents get all the fun with the children and the parents get the work. When we assist an aged parent, we get the work and the grandchildren get the fun. They visit, listen to stories with relish, bring a gift, and then with a smile dash away until the next time. Complaints are reserved for the adult child.

DEALING WITH COMPLAINTS

Nursing parents at home or visiting them regularly, hearing their complaints about care, meals, inability to function as they used to; all this accentuates recognition of our own aging. Erma Bombeck wrote about looking down at her hands and seeing that they were her mother's. Right at the time when parents need our help the most, we are experiencing change ourselves—physical problems (often the beginning of the same ones we see in our parents), career or retirement transitions, widowhood, reduced income, pressure from children needing or due financial help or who have returned to the nest, and even caring for grandchildren.

Because the physical and emotional strain at this time underscores our own aging, we often feel rebellious. Resentment may build toward a parent whom we perceive to be the cause of our present condition. Dr. Archibald D. Hart says, "When unresolved anger is experienced over a period of time, it creates in us a feeling of displeasure and indignation which is called resentment." [1]

To resolve these feelings we must first acknowledge them. If we don't, the anger and resentment increase and cause constant friction in the relationship with a parent.

We must recognize that a parent may have no other outlet for his or her frustration. Though we may be able to share our feelings with a spouse or a friend, most parents put up a good front to visitors, whether they are friends, pastor, or relatives from other areas who visit briefly. They save their discouragement, complaints, and hostility for their children.

We need to forgive our parents. Forgiveness is not

necessarily for some recent incident. We may need to forgive another for an action causing longstanding resentment in us. Because I had so much responsibility for both parents, I recognized that I needed to forgive my mother for having an only child.

Many years before Mother told me she had decided not to have more children. As a little girl, I used to pretend I had an older brother who was away at school; sometimes I "talked" to a pretend sister. Though I always felt loved and wanted, I longed for siblings. This is an interesting thought today when many couples are putting off raising families or planning to have only one child. According to statistics, only children are generally more intelligent, healthier, and have more opportunities for education and development than those from large families. This may be true, but I believe that growing up with brothers or sisters has advantages.

On days when I felt particularly weary, I dwelt on the fact that I had no brother or sister with whom to share concerns. One day, while meditating, the Lord showed me my need to forgive my mother. I wrote the date in my journal. Then, whenever Satan reminded me of my resentment, I stood my ground. "On this particular date," I would say, "I forgave Mother for making me an only child." In time, the resentment left and a deeper love for my mother was a reward for that time of forgiveness.

You may say, "That was a simple thing to forgive, but I had a father who beat me whenever he came home drunk." Or, "I had a mother who disappeared for days at a time." It is true some parents have hurt us physically or emotionally in terrible ways, yet it is not the *degree* of hurt that we measure when we forgive a parent. God used no such yardstick when He sent His only Son to die for us.

Willingness to forgive a parent, and consistently

affirming the decision, eventually results in truly being able to love that father or mother, in feeling more relaxed, more energetic, and better able to carry out duties, to sleep better, and have fewer physical ailments. Forgiveness is purifying, and eliminates the regret that accompanies a lack of forgiveness when it is too late.

In his book *Self-Esteem: The New Reformation*, Robert H. Schuller writes, "Forgiving is living. We'll take a giant step up the let's-feel-good-about-ourselves ladder when we experience the profoundly positive, regenerating, rejuvenating, revitalizing, peace, love and joy that is the emotional reward of the person who receives and offers forgiveness."[2]

DEALING WITH DEMANDS

Mother's demands on my time, especially while she was living with us, were often picayune and excessive. She might call me from one end of the house in the midst of a difficult chore just to have me see a particular person in a soap opera. Or she might keep changing her mind about what she wanted for lunch even though I had it prepared. She would call me to cover her legs with her afghan, a task she was capable of doing for herself. No wonder I felt resentful and weary! But whose fault was that? Not Mother's. That was my problem, and I did not take a stand.

One night I had a dream that expressed this problem. It is well to record a dream immediately before you forget it. Through it you may learn truths about yourself and your relationships, answers to problems, and perhaps hear from God in a creative way. In this particular dream. Mother and I had gone to a Christian Women's Club luncheon (which we often did while she was still able to go out) and had left the table to go to a rest room. I was guiding

Mother, holding her arm just as I always did. The rest room, located on an upper floor, looked out over a large parking lot, and I could see my car parked at the farthest corner of the lot. Mother pointed out the window and said in a gentle voice, "Would you go out to the car and get me a little glass of goat's milk?"

Even in the dream, I felt resentment rising. Here I had taken her to a nice luncheon but she was not satisfied! She wanted me to walk all the way out to the car for a glass of goat's milk! To get goat's milk symbolized her preposterous requests. Just as I was about to "let her have it," a woman smilingly said to me, "The word for today is *kindness*!"

When I awakened, I could still hear her bell-like voice. *Kindness*! "But when the Holy Spirit controls our lives He will produce this kind of fruit in us: love, joy, peace, patience, kindness, goodness, faithfulness" (Gal. 5:22 TLB).

THE FIRM, 'NO'

As I meditated on this dream, I could see that my response to preposterous demands need not be anger or rebellion. If the Holy Spirit was in control of my life, the response could be patient and kind; it could also be a firm *no*.

"No, I am busy now. You may come get yourself a glass of milk if you wish."

"I cannot write that letter today. I'll do it for you tomorrow."

"Is there anything you need now? I shall be busy for the next couple of hours and can't be disturbed."

Why was it hard for me to assert myself, to be firm, to say no? I believe that because Mother never let me forget how much she was giving up to move, I tried to replace all those things—friends and family, church, home, furniture—by responding to her unreasonable and frequent

84

demands. I am sure Mother herself was unaware of her anger at no longer being in control of her life. Unfortunately, both of us lost our natural zest for living during this trying time.

Maturity coupled with kindness effected a dramatic change in the ninety-three-year-old mother of a friend. This aged mother, who was living in another state with her daughter, came to spend some time with her son Dick, who is seventy, and her daughter-in-law, Jean, age sixty-five.

Evidently the daughter harbored bitterness and rebellion in her heart, as she had yelled at her mother constantly, told her off and, in general, behaved rudely toward her. This elderly lady was able to walk, perform simple tasks, and converse rationally; but she was weak, undernourished, and depressed when she arrived.

Jean gave her nutritious meals and a sensible routine. Her person was respected by these two elderly people who cared for her and within a few weeks a noticeable change in her occurred.

As I turned to leave their home one day, Jean told me, "She wants to stay." Of course. Aged people respond to the same sort of care that young children do: love, good food, routine, and discipline.

If a parent comes to live in your home, *begin right* and you will have less cause for guilt, rebellion, and resentment on both sides.

Here are some more ideas to consider:

• *We cannot replace the husband or wife of a parent.* A recently widowed parent will be lonely, but we cannot assuage that loneliness by attempting to replace the one who has died. The desires and interests of our own spouses come first, regardless of the parent's loss. We must be firm about needing privacy. Speaking the truth in love may not be well-received, but that is the parent's problem, not ours.

• *Be a helper, not a slave.* A medical examination of a parent will help to assess real needs. We have not been hired as nurse/companions. We are daughters or sons or in-laws who are willing to help when necessary, to encourage independence when possible. Some parents, however, refuse to be helped at all, and therefore do not bathe or dress properly. Firmness is needed, as well as reminders. Give encouragement and praise for the things they do well.

• *Prepare the parent's room in a practical way.*

Using some of a parent's own furniture enhances feelings of security.

Arrange lighting to best advantage and install a night-light.

Hang a bulletin board for pictures and reminders.

Don't use throw rugs; they're dangerous.

Put up a bed rail. Many old people fall out of bed.

Remove a lock that is installed on the inside of the door to prevent the aged parent from locking you out when you might be needed in an emergency.

However, respect her privacy. All family members should knock if the person's door is closed.

• *Have rules.* Even if this is painful, rules are as necessary in these circumstances as they are for the benefit of children. In our homes, parents must follow family routines, not expecting help at inconvenient times unless it is unavoidable. Be clear in explaining mealtimes, entertaining, and the rights of children who may be living at home.

• *Decisions: Most are ours.* If a parent is ailing enough to need our help at home, he probably needs us to make decisions concerning finances, doctor appointments, and daily routines. Allow a parent to make small decisions, such as buying family gifts, clothing purchases, and snack choices.

If parent care becomes too stressful, consider the options: a nursing home, having the parent visit another relative for a break, or hiring part-time help. Another alternative is to work outside the home and hire full-time help.

Life together in those last years need not be one of frequent conflict. Times of pleasure and joy often break forth spontaneously; other times they need to be planned. If the parent's health permits, encourage sewing, reading, doing crafts, dusting the room, and looking at some TV. Place a comfortable chair outside during pleasant weather, and invite an older friend occasionally to visit alone with a parent.

It is healthy and fulfilling to find common ground that fosters harmony in the family group.

Before my parents were in those last stages of life, they enjoyed family gatherings, watching great-grandchildren play, eating ice cream on the porch, petting the family pets. Having friends in for tea or a snack provided outside stimulation. Giving parents a chore to do—such as preparing vegetables or cracking nuts—provides help and a sense of usefulness for them.

Asking parents to forgive us when we have been irritable and short-tempered smooths the day. Be real. Let go of the past. To give the present and the future to the Lord sounds simplistic, but we can actively will to help ourselves and our parents. "And above all these [put on] love and enfold yourselves with the bond of perfectness—which binds everything together completely in ideal harmony" (Col. 3:14 TAB).

TIME TO CONSIDER

1. Do you acknowledge feelings of resentment? Dr. Hart says this comes from unresolved anger. Do you feel anger toward your parent? Toward siblings who are not helping you? Have you expressed it or repressed it?

2. How can we forgive when we don't feel like it? Are feelings important to an act of forgiveness? What does the author say are the rewards of forgiveness in our lives?

3. Do you have trouble saying no? Why? How can you be a "servant" in the Christian sense and still say no?

4. If your parent lives with you, what is the hardest part of this arrangement? What are the benefits? Do you agree with the author's suggestions for life together? What others could you add?

8

...

Light My Candle

"For thou wilt light my candle: the Lord my God will enlighten my darkness" (Ps. 18:28 KJV).

"He who has the Son has life; he who does not have the Son of God does not have life" (1 John 5:12).

While science and medicine work laboriously to lengthen the human life span and to solve the mysteries of such diseases as cancer and Alzheimer's, many churches are behind in ministering to their elderly. Though some churches have Golden Oldie clubs, Keenagers, and Ageless Wonders, a satisfying program of worship and study is not always given priority over bus trips, crafts, and speakers. All these should be provided, but the depth of need in the lives of some people is not always met.

While in their nineties, two of my father's cousins wrote to me. One finished her last letter with this quip: "I was ninety-one in April and felt fine until I had the fall, but I am working for a comeback. Listen, Dearie, I still have all my teeth. How's that?" This plucky oldster lived alone in her own home. Irene, another cousin, a former schoolteacher and nursing home resident, outlived four pacemakers and wrote: "You don't know how terrible it is to grow old and be good for nothing. I can't see why the Lord doesn't take me as long as my heart is so bad. I hope you can read this terrible writing. At ninety-four it is a wonder I can write at all."

SHARING THE GOSPEL

Actually Irene's writing was more legible than mine, and her mind keen. Though she suffered from painful arthritis, she read daily and asked me theological questions that no one had discussed with her. If science is going to provide the Irenes of our world with pacemakers and pills, then we, the church, should be far more active in sharing with them the Gospel of Christ and how He meets us where we are.

There is a story attributed to President John Quincy Adams who at the age of eighty was asked how he was. He replied, "Mr. Adams is quite all right, thank you. Of course the house he lives in is a bit dilapidated; its walls are tottering on their foundation; its roof is greatly in need of repair. I think he is soon going to have to move out of his old house into another not made with hands. However, Mr. Adams is quite all right, thank you."[1]

Those who say, "I have a private faith," or "I don't talk about my religion," certainly have no biblical basis for such an attitude. It's not the way to turn the world upside down as the early Christians did (Acts 17:6).

Ruth, a tiny lady of eighty-four years, was a resident at the same nursing home as my parents. She had lived most of her life in New York State, but her later years were spent in Florida with her retired doctor husband. A widow, Ruth was frail and barely able to walk, even with help. The first time I saw her, she was reading a paperback from the accumulation of novels neatly stacked beside two pink flowering plants on her windowsill. Ruth had soft white skin over small bones and wore a ruffled, lace-trimmed pink gown. Her lap robe was white sprinkled with pink roses.

During my frequent visits to Mother and Dad, Ruth and I exchanged polite conversation. Though her mind was alert, there was an aloofness or detachment—perhaps even depression. As I continued to visit Ruth occasionally, I noticed a gradual change, a gentle fading. She was served a nutritious drink, as she often refused to eat.

One day while I was praying at home the Lord seemed to ask a question: Have you told Ruth about Me? A little startled, I realized I had never shared my faith or prayed with this elderly lady. In spite of all the paperbacks around her bed, I never saw a Bible.

When I visited the following day, Ruth sat in her usual chair, a closed paperback in her lap. Pale blue eyes watched me as I moved close and sat on her bed. After the general questions had been asked, I took her hand. "Ruth, have you ever accepted Jesus Christ as your Lord and Savior?"

There was a short silence, followed by her soft answer. "No, I don't think I ever have."

"Would you like to?"

Her voice was low, steady, and even a little eager as she replied, "I would. Yes, I believe I would."

"No one can do it for you, Ruth. He is waiting, but you must yield your heart."

"No, no one can do it for you," Ruth repeated. Then, her

91

eyes closed, one tear slowly running down her cheek, she prayed aloud, telling the Lord what He had been waiting to hear. During the following two weeks we spent time in prayer together.

Three weeks later Ruth slipped into a coma. I knelt beside her bed and told her how much she meant to me. I read her the encouraging words of David, the promises of Jesus. There was no response, but I felt she heard.

NEVER TOO LATE

One day I stopped in and the bed was empty. There were no books or flowers on the windowsill. The pink gowns had disappeared from the closet. I had learned a lesson. It may be too late to learn to ride a bicycle or play tennis; too late to learn to drive, to garden, or to swim; but while we still have the gift of life, it is never too late to give ourselves to the Lord. I believe God had waited for Ruth's answer to Him, and then He graciously took her home.

If you are open and compassionate, it will be difficult to restrain your witness to patients in a medical facility. I do not mean to suggest that you wave your Bible and whirl them around in their wheelchairs! As you visit, you will become sensitive to particular people, and the Spirit will show you individual needs.

I met Doris, a prayer warrior, at an intercessors' conference. She told me how she had become a catalyst between her friend Laura and Laura's mother, a nursing home resident with a broken hip. Laura had spent ten years in a mental institution. She had been released, but her complete recovery was blocked by her mother's complaining and accusations. The mother said to her daughter, "People say I don't look like I belong here!" to which Laura replied, "People said that of me when I was in the mental institution, Mother."

The Lord gave Doris His wisdom as she visited this mother, showing her that the resentment over her confinement was harming Laura, who was the only member of the family able to visit her.

I believe this illustrates a point for those of us who make occasional visits to patients in medical facilities. Our brief exchanges do not provide us with knowledge of the entire situation or "both sides of the story." A careless statement may undermine a family relationship that is hanging by a thread. We may agitate the patient or his family; we may promise hope that we are powerless to deliver.

One handsome elderly man, wearing a pin striped shirt and a tie, usually sat in his wheelchair near the entrance of my parents' room. He seemed so accomplished, telling me extravagant stories of his past and present. I listened, assuming that he was wheelchair-bound due to a heart condition. How surprised I was to find one day that he had accosted a nurse with a knife and had escaped from the home! (They found him in a few minutes.) Unless you have been involved for some time with geriatric residents, you may be surprised to find that a person who had responded to you and enjoyed your companionship suddenly refuses to see you or does not know you. In cases such as this, tell the staff about the change in this person: it may be symptomatic of a new illness or organic brain disease.

VISITING OTHER RESIDENTS

Not all residents in a nursing home are over sixty-five. Accidents, muscle and nerve diseases, even strokes, render young people incapable of living independent lives. While my parents were hospitalized, Mike, a twenty-two-year-old construction worker, struggled with therapy, finally leaving for a rehabilitation center to learn a new type of skill that would enable him to be gainfully employed.

The unmistakable odor of roses greeted me one afternoon as I stepped out of the elevator at Medical Care Center. "Roses!" I blurted out, looking for the usual basket sent to the home by the family of a deceased resident.

"Right!" responded a nurse carrying a tray of medications. "Reba's husband sent them to every resident!"

Sure enough, every room was bursting with red blooms. Reba's husband, a florist, showed his caring in the only way he could. His infrequent visits to his wife, a woman about fifty with multiple sclerosis, left her exhausted and frustrated. Usually very quiet, one day she angrily shared with me her resentment toward her husband, tensing her fists and turning her head fretfully on the pillow. All I could do was hold her hand and listen. Reba died after three years in the medical center.

Sam, my father's first roommate, was fifty-eight when brain damage occurred following heart surgery. He was attached to tubes and machines when I met him. Several of us prayed faithfully and praised the Lord as he gradually became independent of the technology that had sustained him. He began to eat, adding flesh to Ichabod-like bones. By the time both my parents died, Sam was able to converse (though in limited ways), walk awkwardly, and spend a few holidays at home. Sometimes I wonder if we stopped praying too soon. Perhaps full recovery was in order. Thoughts such as these can complicate our own emotions and relationships. I decided I could not carry guilt over Sam.

One of the most difficult aspects of visiting a family member in a nursing home is that of visiting others too. I reached a place, for a time, when I could not do so; my own weariness rendered me incapable of coherent exchange with other residents.

Some families never visited other residents even though I knew them to be caring people. Perhaps their loved ones desired every bit of them, every moment they could spare. My mother seemed to feel this way, and I solved it by wheeling her chair into rooms where we would meet both residents and visitors, enhancing interpersonal communion for all of us.

HELP IN THE DYING PROCESS

I met Bertha McCray while she was a private duty nursing assistant for the resident in the room next to my parents. Eventually she would be the one who would nurse my mother through the dying process. I feel certain the Lord put her in my path early so that we could become acquainted.

Doctors trusted Bertha. Her intelligence, expertise, Christian love, and sense of purpose for her own life were evident as she nursed her patients—usually the terminally ill and very elderly. She herself was elderly—a mother and grandmother of many, rightly proud of the accomplishments of her grown children. Soft-spoken and warm, yet efficient, Bertha's long experience with the dying gave her a wisdom and balance for dealing with the families of her patients. Jesus was truly her light: He lightened the darkness of death for many of her charges; and He lightened the grief of loved ones through her ministry.

Throughout her life Bertha had learned instinctively what is now taught: to recognize the various stages of death (denial, anger, bargaining, depression, acceptance); how to care for terminal patients who need the companionship of others during the dying process; how to watch for significant signs (which are not always noted by purely clinical observers).

Mother and Dad liked Bertha. She visited with us

sometimes when her patient was sleeping and often helped nurses with Dad when he became obstreperous and unyielding. From this wise woman I learned much about love, patience, truth, and compassion.

Her commanding presence seemed to quiet unruly patients. They recognized her as an authority figure as well as a nurse. Bertha's Christian witness to others was the life she led and a tenderness that came from regular study of the Word.

"Am I on my last legs?" This was a question my mother asked half seriously, half in jest, each time she had a setback during her last two years of life.

"No not yet!" I would reply, really not knowing when she would lie dying, voiceless, quiet.

After one hospitalization, when a cataract was removed from her eye. Mother suffered a mild stroke, preventing completion of the surgery. But the doctor had removed the worst one first, so she did have partial eyesight after that.

"Am I on my last legs?" came that faint voice, after a fall that cracked her pelvis. Not waiting for someone to help her to the bathroom, she had tried to go it alone, and failed.

"Just a couple of weeks flat on your back and then you'll be better—unless you try to walk alone again." I smiled as I said it.

Dad's attitude during his last two years of life was a practical and thankful one. "I've lived a long time, and hardly ever been sick," he reasoned. Then with a sly glance he would direct his words to Mother. "I didn't drink, smoke, or run around with other women."

Mother answered dryly, "Well, I knew the first two. I'm certainly glad to hear the last one."

My father seemed to have no regrets, none that he talked about. Though his lifelong occupation was not the one of his choosing, he blamed no one and accepted the way his family had shaped his future. He married my mother, knowing he was her second choice. Her first fiance, whose ring she wore throughout her marriage, was killed shortly before their wedding. Dad loved Mother very much, but his temper and demanding disposition clouded this love and produced havoc throughout a frequently stormy relationship. Yet they valued each other in a special way, traveling together, sharing some of the same interests.

VISITS OF PASTORS

Dad seemed to be prepared for death, sure of his eternal future, needing only my frequent companionship and assurance. Both parents welcomed the visits of various pastors who came to share with patients from the Bible, and to pray with them. So pleasing was that to them that I encourage pastors who have the time (or make the time) to visit nursing homes. To that aged generation, often displaced from their home churches, visits by pastors are special.

Hospice nurses Maggie Callanan and Patricia Kelley share clearly and beautifully ways to listen to and relate to the dying. Their book *Final Gifts* explains what they call nearing death awareness and show us compassionate and insightful ways to meet the needs of the dying and interpret their symbolic or hidden messages.[2]

As we are sensitive to the needs of dying parents or friends, we hear their faint cries for light. Sometimes it comes through physical pain or mental anguish; sometimes it is seen in faded eyes, or felt in a tired handclasp. Sometimes it is buried under superficial pastimes or reticence, as it was with Ruth. It is in most of us, if we are aware enough to know the time has come to move from our earth space to another place prepared for us. When we do not have the words ourselves, the Bible does. Comfort, truth, and assurance may be read to those whose candle is dimming.

"I am the Light of the world," said Jesus (John 8:12). And then He told us not to hide our light under a basket (Matt. 5:15). Our instructions are clear. The Holy Spirit gives us the wisdom to show that light. All we need to do is ask.

TIME TO CONSIDER

1. Many people in hospitals or nursing homes are open to prayer and reading from the Word. Are you comfortable sharing the Gospel with others? If not, are you willing to learn how?

2. If your parent is not a Christian, what are some new ways you can express your own faith to her?

3. Does your church have a ministry to the elderly and shut-ins? Is communion taken to those who desire it? How can you encourage this ministry?

4. If your parent is a resident in a nursing home, have you attended a family support group? How could you help a family whose parent has just entered the home? What would you say? Read Colossians 3:12-17.

5. Study the Scripture passage President Adams referred to when he said he will "soon move out of this old house" (2 Cor. 5:1-10). Could you use this to help someone near death? Read verse 10 again. How does forgiveness in Christ take away the fear of dying?

9
...

Forsake Me Not

"In You, O Lord, do I put my trust and confidently take refuge, let me never be put to shame or confusion! Cast me not off . . . in the time of old age; forsake me not when my strength is spent and my powers fail" (Ps. 71:1, 9 TAB).

What pictures come to mind when you read the words "take refuge"? Do you think of a cave, a church, a redwood tree, or the comforting wings of a mother hen? In meditating on this verse I see an open meadow, grass bending in the wind, sun beating down on a treeless plain. When we are helpless and unshielded, God can be our only protection. He is there when we are the targets of anger or criticism. We can have confidence in Him.

When we put our trust in God at an early age, we build a foundation for knowing that in our late years, when our strength is spent and our powers fail, He will not fail us. The psalmist does not say that *our* strength will always be sufficient, or that *our* powers, physical or mental, will not fail; but that we may put our trust confidently in the Lord—and that means in old age too.

While my parents were in the nursing home, my mother usually attended a Bible study taught by a woman who had been a professional singer. She sang favorite hymns for the residents and then opened the Word of God in an insightful way. Although Mother couldn't grasp the teaching, I noticed that the healing properties of Scripture gave her a sense of peace and quiet.

One day while taking the elevator I rode with a plump rosy-cheeked nursing assistant, who was manipulating a wheelchair supporting an elderly lady, Mrs. Nichol. Vacant eyes looked up at me, wisps of gray hair fell over sunken cheeks. Clutched in her arms lay a baby doll, neatly gowned in embroidered lace and wrapped in a pink flannel blanket. I reached out and touched the doll. "How's your baby today?" I asked. I felt a catch in my throat as I re-membered the time I had brought one of my grandchildren, a loving little boy, who climbed into Mrs. Nichol's lap.

"This is *my* baby," I had told her.

She touched Christopher's bare brown leg. "Oh, *your* baby is warm," she observed.

Soon after Mrs. Nichol received her "baby," several other dolls appeared on ladies' laps. As some of the women patients regressed in thought and speech, the dolls seemed to satisfy a yearning.

WHEN FAMILIES AND FACULTIES FAIL

Never, during the years my parents were residents at the home, did I see a member of Mrs. Nichol's family. Perhaps they came. One Christmas, though, gift-wrapped boxes lay on her bedside chair, unopened. Late in the day when Bill and I were returning Mother and Dad to the home after the holiday with us, I heard a nurse say,"Oh, Mrs. Nichol, your presents aren't opened. Come, I'll help you. Here, you pull the ribbon."

One day I arrived to visit Dad at lunchtime. It's wise to visit at different times of the day or evening if you can. He was concentrating on his tray, sprinkling two packets of powdered saccharin over his broiled chicken, baked potato, and green beans. He opened another packet, and covered his buttered bread and dish of dietetic peaches.

"Dad! You're putting sugar on your food!"

"Yep. Tastes better that way."

Mother was stirring her tea. "He always does that," she told me. "I think it's terrible. He's crazy."

He did indeed do it every day, since he did not use the sweetener in his coffee. Perhaps, as a diabetic, he craved sugar.

Once again, I thought about that poem Dad had composed almost fifty years earlier. This same man (who was now mixing his peaches with his beans) had once written:

The inviting green cucumber
Gets most everybody's number
While the green corn has a system all its own;
Its behavior is quite vicious
And a doctor will be coming to your home.

I sank wearily into the plastic chair near Dad's wheelchair. I noticed that the plants on his windowsill had died. I had tried to keep this retired florist supplied with plants, but I stopped when I discovered that the reason for their death was the nutrients they were receiving. Dad was watering them with the contents of his urinal.

101

It was a time when Holy Communion was celebrated in the dayroom, though, that showed me the extent of his mental deterioration. That day, as the wafer was being passed to a circle of patients, my father's face became strangely dark and melancholy. I knelt before him, offering the wafer. He pushed it away. I tried to place it in his mouth. He spit it out. Finally, when I put it in his hand, he tucked it in the pocket of his sweater, which he always wore over his pajamas. "Dad," I whispered, using words I thought he would recognize from his Lutheran prayer book. "Bread of heaven, on Thee we feed, For Thy flesh is meat indeed; Ever may our souls be fed with this true and living bread."[1] He became so agitated that I had to take him back to his room.

I do not pretend to understand his anger and rebellion. Alone in the rest room I wept tears of hurt and frustration. Had I hoped that participating in communion, so often a part of his past, would heal Dad's mind? Had I simply wanted to share in this communion with my aged father? Was it the shock of knowing that he was, in a sense, dead?

IS YOUR FATHER DEAD?

The thought that a senile parent is *dead* is not the same as describing someone as a vegetable (a term I find distasteful and inappropriate). It was a totally new thought to me until a friend said one day in her frank way, "Is your father dead for you?"

Shocked, I heard myself answer, "Yes."

The first state of death begins quietly and is graphically described by Paul Tournier in his book *Learn to Grow Old!*

It is no easy matter to accept that one is growing old, and no one succeeds in doing it without first overcoming his spontaneous refusal. It is difficult, too, to accept the growing old of someone else, of one's nearest and dearest. That of a mother whose kindness, welcome, and understanding used to seem inexhaustible, and with whom one begins to hesitate to share one's intimate confidences, because they no longer arouse in her the warm, lively echo they used to. The aging of a father whose judgment and advice always used to seem so sound, but whom one can no longer consult because he must not be worried, or because his faculties are failing. The aging of a friend to whom one no longer talks as one used to, because it would be necessary to shout loud things that used to be said quietly. It is hard to accept the decay of conversation into banality, empty optimism, and insignificance.[2]

Senile dementia—that's how the doctor described my father's irrational and sometimes inexplicable behavior. The meaning of the words is obvious, but there are many specific types, such as Alzheimer's disease, which must be professionally diagnosed. Named for a German neurologist who first described it in 1906, Alzheimer's is an irreversible brain disorder and the fourth leading cause of death among adults in the U.S. It brings gradual deterioration of memory and intellectual abilities, eventually requiring full-time nursing care.

Scans and X-rays of the brain are essential to differentiate this form of *senile dementia* from depression, anxiety, delusion, cardiovascular problems, or the effect of malnutrition or medication.

Dismissing a parent's confusion, memory loss, or depression as a natural result of age can be an incorrect judgment. It is helpful to find a doctor interested enough in eliminating physical and organic causes before he shrugs his shoulders and gives the condition a general label. I did not do this, probably because of my father's advanced age, and my ability frequently to change his mood or outlook during visits. In addition, as a diabetic, Dad occasionally suffered lapses and metabolic changes causing confusion.

In his book *To Be Old and Sad—Understanding Depression in the Elderly*, Nathan Billig M.D., writes:

Depression in the older adult is complex and involves the biology of aging, the mixture of losses and successes through life, the interplay of medical illnesses and their treatments, and the strengths and weaknesses that make up the person. Depression results from a number of factors and produces diverse symptoms. A comprehensive medical and psychological evaluation is required to make an accurate diagnosis so that a treatment plan can be initiated.[3]

MAKING FINANCIAL DECISIONS

How thankful I was that I had insisted Dad give me the power of attorney while he and Mother were still together in their apartment. The shock of his fall, and Mother's confusion while being moved to our home, rendered both of them incapable of making financial decisions or paying bills. However, this presented a whole new area of responsibility for Bill and me. Some investments were out of state; others were earning very low interest. Dad's records were complete, but complicated. As I studied them, a sort of inflating balloon seemed to rise in my chest, a fearful foreign invader, causing me to feel dizzy and incompetent.

When I prayed about this awesome task for someone of my ability (or lack of it), the Lord assured me that He would see me through. Truly He did, opening the right doors for counseling, showing me that I could indeed be a steward of my parents' resources. Through all those years, as I filled out forms, waited in Social Security offices, transferred funds, and paid bills, the Lord gave me peace and confidence. For many, the mechanics of financial transactions may be a simple task; I had much to learn. I praise God that in our case there were financial resources. For those families whose finances are extremely limited, prayer is the necessary beginning to knowing where to go for help, and how to seek creative options in care.

My father had been a businessman and my mother his bookkeeper. They were frugal people, survivors of the Great Depression. As a child, I remember that when we vacationed by car every penny we spent was recorded. Gas was 18 cents a gallon then, and a spacious apartment rented for $30 a month. What I found to be the greatest stumbling block in my task as power of attorney was conveying to Dad the method I used to manage his finances. Financial terminology had changed as well as his ability to comprehend; inflation, interest rates, and nursing home charges bewildered him further. I was frustrated and insecure when he questioned me.

DEALING WITH CONFUSION

Darkness and confusion began to spread in Dad's mind like a cancer. Stripped of his record books, his wallet, and checkbook, he felt lost and disoriented. One day, as I came in the door, he shouted, "Am I glad to see you!" I never knew what this might portend, for it was a favorite phrase. It meant that something was troubling him, and he looked to me to solve it.

This particular visit occurred some months after Bill and I had sold one house and bought another. Dad had visited our new home in his wheelchair and had dinner with us.

"You know what I think?" he hollered, gripping the

arms of the wheelchair. "That man—that man who lived on a hill—has taken my money and bought a house with it!" (Our former house was situated on a hill.)

"What man, Dad?" I asked.

"That man who bought the house!" His brow wrinkled deeply.

"Do you mean Bill?"

"Yes, yes."

Quietly I reached to take the big hand, now clenched in anger. "Bill is my husband, Daddy, and you know him very well. Now stop and think—do you believe he would take your money?"

The brow relaxed a bit. He touched his chin.

"Bill," I repeated, "your son-in-law. Do you really think he would take your money?"

A little smile played around his lips. It spread sheepishly as he began to laugh at himself. "No, no, I don't think that. I don't know what happens to me. My head gets mixed up, but you always straighten me out!"

Bringing my father face to face with the facts was a constant task. At the time I didn't give it a name, but psychologists call it *reality therapy*.

In order to help my father deal with worries about his finances, I periodically brought him a paper listing his assets, where they were located, and the names of the banks or firms where I transacted his business. He would study them carefully and always thank me profusely. "This has relieved my mind," he would say each time. Later he would not remember that I had brought this accounting, and I would need to do it over again. (It is important not to leave papers or statements with your parents, where they might be misplaced, read by others, or stolen.)

Being without a wallet was very disturbing to Dad. "Suppose they take up a collection here?" he asked me.

"I don't have any money!" Of course large sums could not be left in his bedside table, but I brought a few quarters and put them in his drawer, for which he was very grateful. He never remembered they were there, but if he asked again, I would show them to him, and he would be satisfied. Small ways to relieve anxiety!

Even for those of us not in a confused state, Dr. Archibald D. Hart has a good word in his book *Feeling Free*:

We depend on one another for reality. Whatever else it takes to set our *real* selves free, it can only happen in the context of our relating to one another. There is no way we can become real in isolation. We need people to made it happen. It seems to me that this is how God has ordained it, whether we like it or not. Why else would He have had so much to say about love? And forgiveness? And caring? It is only in our blending with one another that these can happen. . . . Place psychotics in an accepting and understanding community and they get better. Surround an alcoholic with support and caring, and he gives up his alcohol. Communities, we are discovering, can be powerful and therapeutic change agents. . . .

Why should this loneliness and psychological isolation prevent us from becoming real? Primarily because it prevents us from meeting our basic needs in a safe and stress-free manner. We all need to be loved, feel secure, be recognized, and have companionship—and these needs can only be met satisfactorily when we have significant "others" to whom to relate.[4]

JESUS AS YOUR EXAMPLE

You may be the *other* in the life of a now-dependent parent. When attacked unfairly by a senile parent you need to let Christ in you reveal Himself to your parent. Jesus was real with the people He came in contact with. "Daughter . . . your faith has made you well," (Luke 8:48) He said to the woman with the hemorrhage. At the house of a synagogue official, He entered and said directly to the mourners, "Do not weep; she is not dead but sleeping" (Luke 8:52). They laughed at Him, but what did He do? He put them all out and entered the child's room, where He called her back to life.

How directly Jesus addressed the woman of Samaria when they met at the well! Not only did He lead her to confront the reality of her own life, but He told her, "I who speak to you am He (the Messiah)" (John 4:26).

We can learn from our Lord's example how to deal with those around us. By being firm and loving, we can attempt to bring a parent or friend back to the reality of the situation. Pray for dispersion of the darkness in that mind. It is tiring, and it is work, but it is the best way to help our parents and ourselves.

Perhaps an early relationship with a parent has left you without love or respect for him. If you were abused, physically or emotionally; if your parent was an alcoholic, one who neglected his family responsibilities, or tried to rule your affairs throughout your adulthood, your Adamic nature may want to strike out, to pay back or hurt. Beth Ulrich says when she counsels adult children whose parents are hospitalized, she needs to know the family history in order to help people deal with their present stress. "Many adult children were neglected or bullied or hurt in terrible ways," she says, "and now they must resist the desire to hurt back." If you have received new life in Christ, you must will to love that person as Christ loves, praying before each visit with the parent, asking God for the grace, forgiveness, and caring.

Some days Mother responded to my suggestion to go outside to enjoy a spring breeze and the blooming quince or to attend a musical program in the dayroom. On other days her poor circulation and weakening heart caused sleepiness or an altered personality. For several months she frequently "saw pictures on the wall." Often portraying pleasant memories of her past, the pictures included beautiful flowers, handmade quilts, a horse and buggy; sometimes the "Muppets" or a Russian cossack dancer! Telling me about them, she appeared neither frightened nor upset—they seemed to provide entertainment. The doctor called them senile hallucinations.

After visiting her one day when she was particularly foggy, I returned home and wrote:

I came to see you today, Mother
But you weren't there.
You feared this day, and yet,
Now that it's come,
Your spirit is gentle and unafraid.

I came to see you today, Mother,
But you weren't there.
You knew me, and spoke,
But somehow, it wasn't you.
"I saw those pictures on the wall again," you said.
"A man with a plow. A beautiful flower."

I came to see you today, Mother
And we really couldn't talk,
Your world was different from mine.
The man with the plow.
Is he the one Jesus talks about in Luke?
"No man having put his hand to the plow,

109

And looking back, is fit for the kingdom of God."
The flower. Is it a lily of the field?

I came to see you today, Mother,
And though I wept, I won't look back.
I will look forward to your entrance
Into the kingdom.
I bent to kiss you.
"The Lord be with you," I said.
"Oh, He is," you answered, and closed your eyes
For a nap.

"Is your mother dead for you?" The words dared to penetrate my own mind. Yes, as Dr. Tournier said, I no longer shared intimate confidences with my mother, for the response had changed; I no longer asked my father for his advice—now he turned to me. A certain form of death had occurred. As I observed it, I knew that, one day, it could happen to me. Now was the time to meditate upon the words of St. Paul in 2 Corinthians 12:9 "My grace is sufficient for you, for My strength is made perfect in weakness." *The Amplified Bible* reads this way:

But He said to me, "My grace—My favor and loving-kindness and mercy—are enough for you, [that is, sufficient against any danger and to enable you to bear the trouble manfully]; for My strength and power are made perfect—fulfilled and completed and show themselves most effective—in [your] weakness." Therefore, I will all the more gladly glory in my weaknesses and infirmities, that the strength and power of Christ, the Messiah, may rest—yes, may pitch a tent [over] and dwell—upon me!

TIME TO CONSIDER

1. The author refers to the "healing properties" of scripture. What passages come to mind that may bring healing to you or your parent? What psalms are comforting? What passage is your favorite?

2. If your parent exhibits signs of confusion or dementia, has she had a medical evaluation that seems correct to you? How can you find an emotional balance between helping her and helping yourself?

3. What does the author mean by saying her senile parent is "dead" for her? What kind of grief does this cause? Dr. Jane Potter says caregivers often begin to mourn the (Alzheimer's) patient before she dies and that this is a natural reaction. Do you agree?

4. If you are the local caregiver and your siblings live far away, how can you share the changes in your parent? If this is causing a problem, ask her doctor for a written evaluation of her condition that you can share with them.

5. Jesus spoke clearly and directly to people on a one-to-one basis. Read the passages in Luke 8 and John 4 mentioned in this chapter. How can these help in your parent and sibling communication?

10

...

A Mind Set on the Spirit

\

"For the mind set on the flesh is death, but the mind set on the Spirit is life and peace" (Rom. 8:6 NAS).

"I will pray the Father, and he shall give you another Comforter, that he may abide with you for ever" (John 14:16 KJV).

"If we live in the Spirit, let us also walk in the Spirit" (Gal. 5:25).

The man dressed in black stood in the doorway of the church fellowship hall holding a Bible. At the opposite end of the room I was entertaining a church circle with a humorous reading. I was seventeen, a member of the church, and happy to use my speaking talent to entertain those who asked me.

As I finished and the women laughed and clapped, that big Bible was raised high at the back of the hall. "Young woman!" came the thunderous words, "you are misusing the talent God gave you. With that voice you should be reading to us from the psalms!"

I don't remember the reaction of the women there, but I have never forgotten the admonition from that visiting missionary. Not that it made any difference in my life's direction. I went on to study radio and theater, and later television. I played roles in community theater and acted as commentator for fashion shows. My voice was used to persuade people to buy jewelry, cars, and clothes.

Many years later, when I knelt beside Ruth's bed in the nursing home and read the Psalms as she lay dying, I knew what the missionary had meant; I knew then the pain he felt the night he called out to me like an Old Testament prophet.

RESPONDING TO THE HOLY SPIRIT

In his book *Quench Not the Spirit*, Myron Augsburger wrote:

The Spirit has come to guide us into all truth. As we study the Bible, the Spirit brings to bear on our lives new insights that will advance our spiritual growth. We are commanded to grow in grace. Many believers have a prolonged spiritual infancy because they have long quenched the Spirit in suppressing His voice. The old saying applies here, "None is so blind as one who will not see."

The sin of suppressing the Spirit's insights rather than surrendering to them has robbed many a professing Christian of joy in the Lord. Some Christians after 10 or 20 years have less joy and enthusiasm than at the time of their conversion. There are many church members whom God has long sought to lead on into His fullness, who are habitually quenching the Spirit and thus robbing themselves of the fruitfulness of the abundant life.

Quenching the Spirit is a sin marked by complacency, indifference, and being satisfied with the status quo. The Bible refers to this sin as self-righteousness, counting oneself as good enough in his present state. Such persons are closed to further revelation of God's purpose in their lives.[1]

I knew that as a professing Christian the Holy Spirit dwelt within me, but it was many years later when He convicted me of my lifestyle and I asked for the release of His power in my life. No one should feel condemned while reading this account of the Holy Spirit's work in my life. In no way do I mean to judge or criticize Christians whose occupations may be similar to mine at that time. It is not the occupation that is wrong; it is how it fits into God's plan for one's life. God works differently in each of us. Each is a unique creation, able to respond and act in different ways.

Since I grew up in a Bible-oriented church whose ministers preached from the Word, I was without excuse, but not until the early 70s when widespread teaching of the Person and Work of the Holy Spirit reached the corner where Bill and I were planted, did we know something was missing in our lives. The enabling power of the Holy Spirit came at a time when life's tragedies made a painful mosaic of our days. God knew our need, and His timing was perfect.

As we grow older and as we interact with aged parents

and other relatives, the work of the Holy Spirit builds a foundation for grace and wisdom in these relationships.

The late Catherine Marshall in her book *The Helper* listed what the Holy Spirit gives us:

Personal awareness of God's love	The fruit of the Spirit
Conviction of who Christ is	Joy
A message of help to others	Renewal
The right words to speak in times of stress	Guidance from God
Comprehension of the thoughts and mind of God	Healing (except what nature or doctors can give us)
Help in our weaknesses	The ability to set our minds on things of the Spirit
Freedom from slavery to sin's harmful habits	An Intercessor with the Father
Any of the gifts of the Spirit	The pledge of eternal life[2]

Years before the time when I asked the Spirit to control my life, He was in control as part of the Trinity without my acknowledgment. Looking back, I know His guidance and protection were present without my knowledge—which makes God's love even more precious!

Now that we have eight grandchildren, I am aware of

how young we can be and still grasp God's truth. When I was a child, our church traditionally gave its seven year olds Bibles. Before we received them, our minister told us a story: he had visited a parishioner's home, and when he asked for their Bible, it was removed from a bookshelf and *dusted*. Actually, he showed us how the lady blew the dust off the book! "I never want to come to *your* home," he said, "and find that *your* Bible is dusty." I never forgot that, and it was probably the reason I began to read that Bible every night when I was eleven. Later, I would understand Jesus' words. "The cares of this world, and the deceitfulness of riches choke the word, and he becomes unfruitful" (Matt. 13:22).

WALKING IN THE SPIRIT

When we belong to the Lord, are filled with the Spirit, and live in the Spirit, the Bible says we should also walk in the Spirit. To me this means that my steps are "ordered by the Lord" and as I submit to Him and to my understanding of His Word and His guidance through prayer, I can step out in faith and trust Him to accomplish His plan.

To honor our parents without feeling guilt over our relationship with them is not only possible, it is healthy and desirable. The Holy Spirit will give us the qualities we need to establish this kind of decisiveness—the ability to forgive, to order priorities, to assess and care for true needs. By comparing our qualities with the fruit of the Spirit (Gal. 5:22), we know whether or not we are walking in the Spirit. However, if we see ourselves lacking this fruit there is no reason to condemn ourselves. Christ died for the ungodly, and we stand clean before the Father, as Jesus intercedes for us. When we meditate on that fact it truly produces joy.

The Holy Spirit guides us in different ways: He protects

us, He gives us wisdom, and He moves us into God's plan for our lives with His power.

Several years ago, I was driving home at dusk with three ministers who had gone to a meeting opposing the building of an abortion center in a nearby city. As I rounded a sharp turn, a voice called in my ear, "Slow down! Slow down!" Obediently I put my foot on the brake, throwing my passengers forward; but as we rounded the turn, there, directly in front of us, was a farm tractor inching along without lights. Traveling at normal speed, we would have crashed into the vehicle. No one else heard the voice, but if I had dismissed or ignored it, disaster would have resulted.

How often we have said, "I don't know what to do." And we don't. At the time I had to decide whether or not to move my mother from our home to a medical care center, the Spirit provided wisdom.

We all have those times when we ask, "Is it my own flesh, my own desires? Is it Satan trying to influence me?" Not easy, is it? But we are not dependent on ourselves. Sometimes as we ask His guidance, He simply answers, *wait*. I know in my spirit when I hear that word. I prefer not to hear it, but when I obey and wait He provides the answer at the right time, and I am spared the entanglements and string pulling that we humans do to effect what we think is the answer to our questions. Sometimes the answer is *act*! It truly helps to have a spouse or prayer partner confirm what we have heard from the Lord.

God knew that Bill and I desired to know Him in a deeper way. I believe that is why we got our unmistakable marching orders to go to the Holy Land. We were part of a fellowship group, some of whom were planning to go on a trip sponsored by the New Directions Ministries of Burlington, North Carolina. At that time both my parents were residents of the nursing home. As an only child, I had repeatedly stated that I would never leave the country while my parents were living. One night at the dinner table Bill and I were discussing the trip which would include Egypt and Jordan, as well as Israel.

Suddenly in the midst of our discussion we looked up at each other, forks in mid air. "Why, we're talking as though we are going, aren't we!" We were astonished. Someone else had made that decision for us. And truly, He had. A mountaintop experience, the trip added an incomparable spiritual depth and luster to our lives. For many reasons, we see now that if we had not recognized the Holy Spirit's guidance at that time, we would probably never have made that trip. Every door was opened for us. I never had a fear or moment of hesitation when we planned the trip or while we were away. His peace came as we followed God's direction and operated in His will.

THE GUIDANCE OF THE HOLY SPIRIT

Two weeks and three days after our return from Israel, my father died. Yes, we had gone in God's timing.

We can make good decisions on our own by assessing various possibilities and weighing alternatives. Excellent secular books are available on a wide variety of subjects designed to change our lifestyles and help us become more mature and able to make sensible and realistic decisions and choices, but as Christians we learn to rely ultimately on the guidance of the Holy Spirit, which is far superior to human wisdom.

By reading Scripture with a listening ear and an open heart, by using the mind God has given us, and in some cases receiving a confirming word from another, we can exercise our God-given "uncommon" sense in decision making. Sometimes, of course, we do not make good decisions in spite of trying to do as God directs. Everything we do does not turn out perfectly, but we can trust that God's hand is in it (Rom. 8:28).

Some of us act rashly according to immediate needs and should recognize that trait in ourselves by slowing down and asking God to step in. Others have the opposite problem—not being able to make decisions. If this is a regular occurrence, we need to get to the root of our inability to make decisions. Sometimes this requires professional help, but for most of us, sorting out priorities is the answer. Even though one particular aspect may seem urgent, it is not always the important one. If Christ has set us free, we should be free from what others think (that is, free to be ourselves in Christ, though others may not agree with our decisions). If we aren't, frustration will set in and bind us with its aggravating cords.

RELIEF FROM STRESS

Because of stress from the uncertain economy and current lifestyles, the world offers various means of relaxation, such as yoga, Eastern meditation, hypnosis, astrology, and various combinations of New Age philosophy. As Christians, we know that none of these constitutes a favorable answer. Some actually bring people to mental breakdown, demon possession, or at the very least, false hopes. Christian meditation, however, focused on Scripture, brings life and peace.

We need to know God. But the wonderful part is that He knows us, and as we seek Him, He shows us how to deal with stress. Over and over in the Bible we are told to ask, to seek, to knock. Instead, we flounder around like a tired swimmer who has gone out too far. Dr. R. Maurice Boyd says, "God will meet me at every corner. He is already there. The future is already filled with God!"[3] What a wonderful thought! Not only is God here with me now, but he is AHEAD of me.

While my parents were in the nursing home, I was able to appropriate short times of rest and relaxation. Sometimes before visiting, I would sit for ten minutes in the lobby, eyes closed, consciously relaxing muscles tensed by working and driving. Other times, while Mother sat in her recliner and Dad in his wheelchair, I stretched out on the bed, removed my shoes and read my mail. If you think you are not free enough to behave this way, try it anyway! You may find that a relaxed presence can often do much for a parent, while giving you time to rest, and allowing you the opportunity to assess the general routine of care.

On several occasions one parent was hospitalized while the other remained in the nursing home, and I needed to visit two places. Because I am able to doze quickly and be refreshed (truly a gift from God!) I would park my car and rest my arms and head on the steering wheel, drifting and dozing, unwinding the tenseness of the body and the whirling of my mind. Then the Spirit could minister to me, much the same way Elijah was refreshed under the juniper tree. Doing this before each visit kept me in one piece.

These ways may not be helpful to everyone. Maybe you'd rather park a distance away from the hospital (as I did occasionally) and relax by walking briskly between car and hospital. Doing stretching exercises, or aerobics, or reading something totally new may be relaxing. Listening to tapes in the car may pave the way for a visit. Whatever the choice, do it! Work it into the time frame of your lifestyle.

Almost two years after Dad's death, I reached a plateau of distress. Mother and I both needed a change beyond our brief time outside on the patio. The sameness of her room, the meals, the tedium of existence threatened to overwhelm both of us. Our relationship was deteriorating due to the state of her physical and mental health and my weariness. Then, true to my impulsive nature, I decided to look at another nursing home, more costly, but newer and different, with changes I felt would be beneficial to both of us. I toured, I talked, I listened, I counseled with my husband. Then I sat to pray. I made the decision to move Mother, even knowing the change might confuse her further.

The very next day, when I began the necessary paper work, my mother suffered a massive stroke. She was never moved. She remained in the same bed, with the people who knew her best caring for her. Five weeks later she died.

I am convinced that when we walk in the Spirit to the extent that we understand and grasp that walk, God honors our individual personalities, answering according to our needs and His will through His bountiful mercy and wisdom.

TIME TO CONSIDER

1. Think of ways God was directing your early life without your realizing it. Do you see symbols or situations He used to guide you? What are they?

2. Read over the list of the ministry of the Holy Spirit by Catherine Marshall. Can you find a Bible verse that underscores each one? (For example, "Help in our weaknesses"—2 Cor. 12: 9, 10).

3. What are the fruits of the Spirit? (Gal. 5:22). Which ones do you have? What ones do you lack? Which ones help you the most in parent care and relationships? Why?

4. Read Acts 20: 22-24 in the New International Version. Paul says he is "compelled" and "warned" by the Holy Spirit. Have you experienced either of these situations? What were the results?

5. What does the word "stress" mean to you? What ways help you to "relieve stress" in your daily life? If you had one day completely to yourself, what would you do?

6. Read all of John 14. Then write out a prayer for yourself based on this chapter and offer it to Jesus.

11

...

A Heart May
Be Happy

*"A good name is better than good ointment, and the day
of one's death is better than the day of one's birth. It is better
to go to a house of mourning than to go to a house of
feasting, because that is the end of every man, and the living
takes it to heart. Sorrow is better than laughter, for when a
face is sad, a heart may be happy"* (Eccles. 7:1-3 NAS).

Death's shadow came suddenly in my paternal grandparents' home. At age eighty-nine, Grandpa had been
bedridden only a few days. Twelve hours before he died,
Grandma's stroke took her quickly. I recall the community's
astonishment at the deaths of the couple only a few hours
apart. There was a double funeral, which I recall, though I
was only seven.

Most of our great-grandparents and even grandparents

died in their own homes—nursed, bathed, and fed by a succession of relatives from the large families who lived nearby. Today oxygen, tubes, catheters, and respirators are used in the green-toned corridors of mercy where most people die.

In addition to contending with the grief and perhaps anger and guilt at the time of a parent's death today, often we must comfort aged people at the doorway of death. Our minds are confused by the accounts of euthanasia and with such phrases as "death with dignity" and "quality of expected life." We know God as the giver and taker of life, and we question the distinctions between ordinary and extraordinary means of sustaining life.

Professor Paul Ramsey wrote:

Why not say that the classification *ordinary/extraordinary* can simply be reduced to: (1) a determination either of the treatment indicated or that there is no treatment indicated in the case of the dying and (2) a patient's right to refuse treatment? The answer to that question is that there are medically indicated treatments (these used to be called ordinary) that a competent conscious patient has no moral right to refuse, just as no one has a moral right to deliberately ruin his health. Treatment refusal is a relative right, contrary to what is believed today by those who would reduce medical ethics to patient autonomy and a "right to die."

In this connection we need to recall that the reasons alleged to warrant refusal or extraordinary treatments were worked out in times that were medically primitive. Because of progress in medical practice, more and more extraordinary treatments have today become ordinary. These are surely medically indicated and desirable.[1]

UNDERSTANDING THE ETHICS

Medically and legally I have no expertise in making these decisions. I have tried to understand these ethics in terms of the familiar: my parents and others I have observed. My father lived to be ninety-four only because he had daily injections of insulin; occasionally he suffered insulin shock, requiring emergency care. Today the diabetic's treatments are *ordinary* and to refuse my father his insulin dose, whatever his age or condition of health, would be morally offensive. In contrast, I learned of a ninety-six-year-old lady taken to the emergency room in heart failure. Employing CPR (cardiopulmonary resuscitation) caused her several broken ribs, and a few weeks of increased suffering before death. I see no reason why a lady of that age should not be allowed to die of heart failure without the resuscitative means available today.

In his book, *Euthanasia is Not the Answer*, David Cundiff, M.D. writes, "Physicians consider the following factors when determining what is ordinary and what is extraordinary treatment:

• Usual vs. unusual treatment for a given condition
• Simple vs. high-tech treatment
• Invasive (such as surgical) vs. noninvasive treatments (such as medication)
• Inexpensive vs. expensive treatments
• Conservative vs. high-risk or long-shot therapies"[2]

Because there is more medical technology, because people are living longer and because there are more regulations as well as moral ambiguities, making decisions at the end of a parent's life is harder, particularly if the parent has indicated no written or verbal advance directive.

RECEIVING WISDOM AND COUNSEL

Rather than feeling overwhelmed by your responsibilities and judgments, remember that first, God gives wisdom; second, there is abundant counsel available today for elders and their children. Your attorney, a hospital social worker, or organizations such as AARP can provide you with information. For example, the Patient Self-Determination Act became federal law in 1991. Every hospital or nursing home must provide at the time of admission written information on an individual's rights under their state law to make decisions regarding medical care, including the right to accept or refuse treatment and the right to formulate advance directives. To wait until a time of emergency admission makes this extremely stressful. If you can, do this in advance or advise your parent to do so.

While few people want their lives prolonged in the dying process, warnings come from many ethicists that euthanasia could become legal just as abortion did. We have only to witness the news about doctor-assisted suicide. We hear about medical rationing as the population ages (realizing, however, that in order to provide our children with proper medical care, this may be a consideration).

Dr. C. Everett Koop, former United States Surgeon General and a committed Christian, says, "The cost of caring for people over sixty-five is eight times the cost of caring for people under sixty-five. And the largest part of that is in the last year of life. So we're going to have to teach people to have a certain tolerance for the problems that come with old age. We must also teach people that when you're eighty-two and coming to the end of this life, you don't have to spend $500,000 to hold on for two more weeks."[3]

Allen Jay, M.D., a member of the bioethics committee for the San Diego Medical Society, gives us definitions of two forms of euthanasia. He says, "Involuntary euthanasia is killing a person without his consent though competent. Non-voluntary euthanasia is the killing of an individual who is not competent to understand what is happening to him."

He cites a moral form of "double-effect euthanasia" as the concept of a physician giving a large dose of medication for the purpose of relieving pain in terminal illness, with the unplanned result that it shortens the patient's life.[4]

This is a complicated issue which we cannot discuss at length here, except to say that there are medically indicated procedures or reasonable therapy to *ease* rather than *prolong* life for the terminally ill or the voiceless dying aged.

RELATING TO THE PARENT'S DOCTOR

An understanding relationship with your parent's doctor is important. If you are one of several children scattered around the country, you may get phone calls that ask: "What does the doctor say?" If possible, establish good communication with the physician before the time comes when you have to make decisions concerning the type and amount of medical interference you and the doctor will allow. Know what shapes the doctor's ethics. When a parent is moved so that he may live with you or near you, it is sometimes difficult to find the kind of physician you would like. At least know how he or she responds to geriatric illnesses.

A question you may ask yourself that will help you and the doctor assess the method of care for your parent at the time of extreme illness is, AM I, BY THIS ACTION PROLONGING THE PROCESS OF DYING, OR AM I, BY THIS TECHNOLOGY, PRESERVING LIFE?

The concept of the hospice has been increasingly employed as a means to minister to the dying. In addition to painkillers and comfort care, an important aspect is the setting in which the dying person can be heard and loved. This compassionate approach may be adopted by you and other caregivers during the dying process of your loved one.

Hospice programs exist throughout the country. The emphasis is on keeping the patient at home, with family, friends, and visiting professionals involved in care. Some hospice programs are hospital-based units; others are in nursing homes or in separate facilities. New insurance coverage (federal and private), as well as other aspects of hospice, make this an attractive option for care. Most patients are those with cancer or are assessed to have six months or less to live.

THE IMPORTANCE OF FORGIVENESS

Love, not guilt, should be the motivating force when you walk through those dark valleys. Hopefully there is time in your life, even now perhaps, to forgive your parent and forgive yourself for the hurts of the past. Forgiving brothers and sisters is important, too, for resentment and anger toward siblings often surfaces at the time of a parent's serious illness.

During the last few months of Dad's life, he positioned his wheelchair at the entrance of his room, looking for me. When I walked toward him, his face would exhibit confusion, fear, and desperation. The nurses' reports were bad. He did not know where he was. He kicked them while they dressed the unyielding ulcer on his leg or administered insulin. He spit out his medication. His pills were crushed and mixed with fruit, and a male CNA helped during treatment times. He no longer read a newspaper or talked about the cars outside his window.

He was sure no one was paying his bills. "We can't afford this motel!" he shouted, distressing Mother. He thought his wheelchair was a car or truck and that he was delivering flowers. Words escaped him. An ambulance was a "hurry-up wagon." Pushing him back to his room did not help, for he became hyperactive and agitated.

Then came the day of God's grace, soon after our return from Israel. Dad was quieter that day, pensive, eyelids fluttering as he sat by the window. Suddenly he brightened.

"I can see it!" he called out happily. "There are special rooms for children."

Thinking he was referring to the parochial school in sight of his room, I answered, "Oh, the school over there."

"No! No!" he insisted. "There's a place for everyone, but you can't enter on the ground floor!"

The Holy Spirit illumined my heart. "Dad," I asked, "do you mean the place where Jesus said, 'In my Father's house are many mansions' and He was going to prepare a place for us?" (John 14:2 KJV).

"Yes, that's it!" He was joyful.

Malcolm Muggeridge, author, lecturer, and novelist, once said it this way:

When you're old, as I am, there are all sorts of extremely pleasant things that happen to you. For one, you realize that history is nonsense. But the pleasantest thing of all is that you wake up in the night and you find that you are half in and half out of your battered old carcass. It seems quite a toss-up whether you go back and resume full occupancy of your mortal body, or make off toward the bright glow you see in the sky, the lights of the city of God.

In this limbo between life and death, you know beyond any shadow of doubt that, as an infinitesimal particle of God's creation, you are a participant in God's purpose for His creation, and that that purpose

131

is loving and not hating, is creative and not destructive, is everlasting and not temporal, is universal and not particular. With this certainty comes an extraordinary sense of comfort and joy.[5]

DAD'S FINAL DAYS

A few minutes after his vision of the rooms, Dad dozed off, his forehead unwrinkled, lips relaxed, gnarled hands folded over his patchwork lap robe.

During the next few days a dark terror again seized my father. The sunlight from heaven disappeared behind the clouds of darkness as Dad argued, fought, and insulted everyone, causing Mother to retreat into sullenness and sleep. I asked our daughter Claire if she could agree to pray with me for Dad's release in death. She said she could. Three days after our agreement, the nursing home held a Memorial Day picnic complete with hot dogs, hamburgers, and balloons. The cooks wore gala hats and aprons.

As I helped residents on the warm breezy patio, a nurse pushed my father's chair toward me. Within a few minutes, after refusing all food, he became ill and was rushed back to his room. Two days later, at 7:30 in the morning the doctor phoned to tell me my father had just died.

"Praise the Lord," I said evenly.

"Yes," said the doctor.

Two funeral services were scheduled: one in Lynchburg, for the benefit of my mother and our children, and another in Utica where he was buried. During the service I shared the story of Dad's vision of the rooms. My face was sad, but my heart was indeed happy, for my confused father had entered that specially prepared place, and God had been gracious enough to let me know it.

A year and a half later Mother suffered a severe "cardiovascular accident," and entered the process of dying.

THE PROCESS OF DYING

Paul Ramsey's book, *Ethics at the Edges of Life*, asks the question:

How can the *process of dying* be identified? How do you know that an infant or a comatose patient is dying? I do not. The reply must be that this is a *medical* judgment and that physicians can and do determine—in human, no doubt fallible judgment— the difference between dying and nondying terminal patients. In the case of those whose death is impending, further attempted salvic treatment can only prolong dying. In the case of nondying terminal patients, however, care calls for making treatment available to sustain them even when this only improves their condition or adds meager life to their days. Both the dying and the incurable if conscious and competent have, in addition, a right to refuse treatment or, better said, to participate in the choice of their treatment (including the choice of no further attempted cures).[6]

If a parent is in this dying process (whether he is fifty or ninety), honoring him means employing biblical ethics bathed in the purest kind of love. This is no small order. This kind of love is the caring love of Jesus. If we have worked through our forgiveness, been relieved of our guilt, and cast our burdens on the Lord, we are ready.

Dolly Pugh, a caregiver to two elderly relatives, serves as an ombudsman on a nursing home council. One resident shared with Dolly her concern about her unforgiveness of a particular relative. "Perhaps she's never been able to unburden herself before," says Dolly. The "comfort care" we provide frail or dying people gives them opportunity to

133

share fearful, painful, or repressed feelings or acts, and gives us the opportunity to minister to them in Jesus' name.

WE SUFFER TOO

Much of the real suffering that goes on during the dying process of a loved one is ours, not the patient's. As a parent nears the entrance to the city of God, we view "the battered old carcass." It may seem that the spirit has almost slipped from the body, leaving a shell. The spirit may be anxious to leave, but those very organs that were formed in the first few weeks after conception are still working to preserve life.

The ordinary treatment for my mother included pureed foods and liquid administered orally with a feeding syringe (usually by Bertha, who took all the time needed and talked gently to Mother). Nearby, like a soldier on guard duty, stood an oxygen tank for those times when her breathing became labored. After two weeks, the doctor ordered a catheter. All these procedures provided sustenance and as much comfort care as possible. As the days stretched out, Mother was able to receive less food and liquid: Bertha documented the intake.

"Look," a young CNA said to me, "her skin isn't resilient." She pinched up some skin on Mother's arm. "She's dehydrating. She needs an IV."

Though the doctor did not suggest or encourage this, I knew I could insist on a naso-gastric tube. This would not bring life back to Mother's eyes or mind; it would not restore movement to paralyzed limbs, it would prolong the dying process. As long as Mother was able to take some liquid by mouth, I decided I would not insist upon tube feeding.

After Lloyd L. Tyndall's wife died of cancer, he wrote a letter to his friends and supporters and has given permission to share a portion of it with you:

At her earthly death I learned a very important lesson I feel I must share. I had been encouraging Shirley to hang on and as a result she was struggling to do so. Finally the hospital chaplain spoke to me.

"You love her very much, don't you?"

"Yes, I do," I answered.

"You know she is suffering by fighting for every breath because you are asking her to," he said. I nodded.

Then he asked, "Are you ready to let her go?"

"Yes," I said.

"Have you told her that?" he asked.

"No," I admitted.

"Don't you think you should?" he asked.

"Yes," I answered.

I returned to her room, kissed her, and told her how much I and the children loved her. I assured her that we were there, and that we were going to be all right. This was her greatest concern, that we would not be able to face what she had already prepared for. I then told her, "Honey, you can go now, if you want to." She totally relaxed, took one breath, and was gone.

Later the nurses told me that letting her go, that giving her permission to die, was the greatest gift I could have given her.

I experienced something similar with my mother. As I held her hand unaffected by the stroke, I asked her questions, but she was unable to squeeze my hand. I stroked her face and told her I thought she could hear me. "I know this must be so hard, not to be able to answer me. I believe you can hear me. Can you?"

Slowly her lips formed one slurred word: "Sure!" I felt so encouraged that I began to sing one of her favorite hymns, "Love Divine, All Loves Excelling." Now I knew she was not imprisoned in an impenetrable darkness; the Word of Life could be administered along with oxygen and water! One of the greatest mistakes family and medical personnel make, in my opinion, is to treat the patient as though she is comatose or absent, when indeed she often hears what is said in her presence.

Part of my suffering during this time were the wrenching changes. My emotions were stretched to accept death, then stretched to accept life again. Three times a call came from the nurse that death was imminent. I rushed off, only to find Mother rallying, holding on to the last thread of life that she loved so much. As she lingered, appearing to be in a place of suffering, I bent over and whispered, "Dear, can you just let go? It's all right if you do. Can you let go to Him?" Whether or not she heard me, I don't know; but two days later, she did let go, into the arms of her Savior.

"Casting all your care on Him, for He cares for you" (I Pet. 5:7). We rejoice and do not weep, for death is a part of life, controlled by our Heavenly Father. We are upheld by His omnipotent hand.

TIME TO CONSIDER

1. What childhood memories do you have of death? How do they affect you today?

2. How does death differ today from biblical times? From fifty years ago? What makes death easier today? Harder?

3. If you are your parent's primary caregiver, have you

discussed her feelings about treatment for serious or terminal illness? In your case, is it wise to do this? If it is, how would you approach the subject?

4. Why is it important to let go of resentment or guilt before a parent is dying? Read Matthew 6:14, 15 and I John 1:9, 10. In addition to "doing the right things," how can this help you deal effectively with parent care and your parent's death? What benefits will you receive?

5. If you are a long-distance adult child, think of ways you can help your sibling caregiver. Is financial help needed or expected? Can you take vacation time to relieve the caregiver? Understand the nearby caregiver may resent your "independence" from the situation.

12

...

What Does the Lord Require?

"He has told you, O man, what is good; and what does the Lord require of you but to do justice, to love kindness, and to walk humbly with your God?" (Mic. 6:8 NAS).

I have often thought of the truth of the doctor's words, "You can provide for your mother's comfort, but not for her happiness."

Whether a parent assumes any responsibility for his or her own happiness under the new conditions in her life, is another story.

Usually it is our parents' comfort and safety that we are concerned about first. We see these old people, now our responsibility, faltering. They had an auto accident that is their fault; they consistently leave the stove burner on and forget their medications; their dishes and clothes are not washed clean, or they skimp on meals. Memory losses intensify; handling money is a mountainous chore.

"How can Mom be safe in this house? The neighborhood is going downhill—two people were robbed last week."

"How can Dad make it through the winter? He turns the heat down so low I'm afraid he'll freeze."

"Mom's eyesight is getting so bad she took the wrong pills yesterday!"

We feel the need to provide for parents whose comfort and safety are in jeopardy. Should something devastating occur, we would feel responsible and guilty that we had not acted sooner. And so, when we see these changes in the lives of a parent or parents, we know that something must be done to protect them from possible harm, and to relieve our consciences.

THE BEGINNING OF CHANGE

When an incident occurs suddenly, such as a fractured hip, there is not time to think through the options. If you are the nearest child, you will probably take charge, moving your parent to a hospital and notifying other brothers or sisters after the fact.

Perhaps, though, the change is more subtle. Mary, for example, calls her mother from hundreds of miles away and finds her unable to hear or respond coherently over the phone. She calls her brother Tom, who lives ten miles from mother. He, too, has noticed changes in mother, and the discussion begins.

Siblings may disagree as to what is the best solution, sometimes basing their decisions on their own emotional or financial needs, rather than determining the most feasible solution in the light of the parent's real needs. In the community there may be choices which will keep that parent in her home: cleaning help, a visiting nurse, Meals-on-Wheels, regular home health care. The local commission on aging, the Mental Health Association, Family Service Agency, Human Services Department, a hospital social worker, or a pastor usually know what services are available locally. These vary from state to state, from urban to rural community, but current awareness of the problems of the elderly has spawned some kind of help in every area. For example, the Central Virginia area agency on aging's homemaker program is one way to help older people stay in their own homes and live their own lives. Often it is the contact with CVAAA that uncovers other needs for service, such as home-delivered meals and a program for low-income elderly to find physicians who will accept Medicare.

State and federal governments often operate in tandem. The homemakers under CVAAA are part of the Virginia Department for the Aging network that receives a large share of its money through the federal Older Americans Act.

Even in largely rural areas, there are solutions. Near Adams, New York, a small community close to the Canadian border, a middle-aged couple run a board-and-care home for eight to ten elderly or handicapped people. They all enjoy country cooking around a large table in the farm kitchen; a comfortable sitting room, plus their own bedrooms with their own furniture; a caring atmosphere where medications and baths are supervised. I visited this farmhouse where a mentally handicapped uncle had settled in. Among the boarders were an aged mother and her middle-aged Down's syndrome daughter. The soothing atmosphere that combined the smell of good food, comfortable chairs, television, pets, and above all, the cheerfulness of its owners, opened my eyes to the possibilities of special care for those facing "in-between places" in life. It takes gifted, energetic people with a love for the less fortunate to provide such care. The cost was far less than a nursing home. However, not all board-and-care homes are licensed or regulated, which is a federal requirement for all nursing homes.

It is well to avoid extreme changes before they are necessary. When change in a parent is gradual, by all means seek the available agencies in that community that provide help to the parent in his or her own home or apartment. Take the next step when it becomes necessary.

If for example, Meals-On-Wheels or a home health care worker can meet an immediate need, try it, though your parent may not appreciate your decision. There may be great resistance to a stranger coming into the home to bring meals, give baths, or clean house. Your parent may say, "But *you* could do this for me." The elderly parent does not always remember that the son or daughter has a full-time job, teenagers at home, poor health, or a combination of all three! I sometimes found that appealing to my parents' love for me helped a great deal. "This would be such a relief to *me*. Would you just try it?" Other times real firmness is needed as you explain that the other option might be leaving their home.

If no child lives near the parent who is failing, an information and referral service or Social Services Department in the community may be able to provide names of organizations that can help. If your parent is reluctant to call, you may need to make the contact and see what measures can be taken.

If your parent can no longer live alone, today's choices vary widely. Location, finances, and type of need will determine your final decision. Some of today's possibilities include shared housing (the Shared Housing National

Resource Center provides information on agencies around the country that sponsor shared residences), group homes, board-and-care homes, and condominiums. Retirement communities offer different levels of care and assistance. Some require a hefty upfront fee as well as monthly charges. Others have no initial fee or lease.

"Life-care" communities are very popular for those who can afford them, offering various residences, such as apartments, one-family cottages, and personal care rooms. Most have health care connected facilities. Be sure to obtain a thorough knowledge of their finances (some have gone bankrupt), contracts, upfront charges, and levels of care. Ask for a disclosure statement and enlist the help of an attorney or accountant.

MAKING DECISIONS

As a Christian, your relationship with the Lord will greatly help you in your decisions. Spend enough time with Him alone to hear what He is saying. If you are married, consult with your spouse; if you are in the habit of praying together, this is a strengthening factor in decision-making. Some praying spouses agree to pray separately for a few days; then they come together to share what they have heard. If the answer is the same, they move ahead with confidence. If not, they talk it over, write down options, and pray again.

Probably no aspect concerning parental care in the later years is as devastating and widespread as money decisions. In their book, *You and Your Aging Parent*, Barbara Silverstone and Helen Kandel Hyman wrote:

Money and material possessions—the abundance as well as the lack of both—very often provide the real underlying source of family dissension. Brothers and

143

sisters have been competing over inheritances since the beginning of time. They are still doing it today, especially when their elderly parents have sizeable estates to leave behind. But even when there is little money and only a few material possessions, these can still assume great symbolic worth. The struggle to win them may be out of all proportion to their value. "Mother's leaving me the silver candlesticks because I'm the oldest," or "I should get the candlesticks because I've done the most for Mother." "Doing" for Mother therefore is expected to pay off. But will this kind of "doing" really pay off for her?

Money can cause trouble when there is none. If Mother is barely scraping along on her small pension and Social Security checks, and her children are in a better financial position, who is going to contribute and how much? Should they all contribute equal amounts? Or should the contributions be from each child according to his emotional need? Will the contribution be given out of generosity or guilt? Will the gifts have strings attached? Will Mother have to subordinate her own wishes to the wishes of the biggest checkbook?

Money is therefore power: "I give Mother the most, therefore I have the right to decide what plans we should make for her." Does money ever buy that right? Many brothers and sisters say no.

Silverstone and Kandel also touch a nerve when they talk about the psychological replacement value that money holds in the emotions of some adult children.

Money can also be a substitute. A son who says, "I send my father a monthly check," may feel he has thereby discharged his total responsibility. Does his monthly check balance out equally with the brother's weekly visit or sister's daily phone call? They may feel that their contributions have greater value, and no amount of money is a substitute for care and concern. Finally, money can become a contest. Competitive brothers and sisters who have money themselves may lavish luxuries on their elderly mother or father, not because either parent needs these gifts or even wants them, but to demonstrate which child has achieved the greatest worldly success.[1]

If the change in your parent's condition requires the help of someone else to handle finances, you should consult a lawyer or legal aid service. If your father trusts you or a sibling enough (trust sometimes turns into suspicion in old age) to grant durable power of attorney or durable power of attorney for health care, it may save you a painful court procedure at a later date. Such legal rights vary from state to state and are best determined by the caregiver in cooperation with a lawyer. A pastor or social worker may be needed to help with the change of a power of attorney.

When a child does not exercise power of attorney soon enough, a mentally incompetent parent may be bilked by unscrupulous people, write checks for services never rendered, or give away family heirlooms as payment for running errands or mowing the lawn. Firmness along with love and consistency are needed to deal with a parent whose body and mind are functioning poorly.

LOVE AND COMMON SENSE

Making decisions about family possessions is a touchy area for all concerned. You might encourage your parent to give away some things that would be appropriate for family weddings or graduations (with your assistance). Approach the matter of sorting and giving *some* things away in a spirit of love and common sense.

Wouldn't *she* rather be the one to decide on dispersement rather than have others sorting her things? Many old people cannot resign themselves to the act that change will occur—for all of us. Siblings (of your parent and yourself) might be called together to make some of these decisions but no matter what you do or decide in the division of material possessions you may be criticized.

Parents who are failing physically or mentally see themselves as losing control of their lives. Role reversal shakes both generations. Communication breakdowns are common at a time when decisions on help, finances, or moves must be made in haste and anger. Real communication requires willingness to listen to one another.

Intermediaries often help. As in the case of my father's driving, his doctor's advice was heeded when mine was ignored. Bring in a pastor, social worker, attorney, physician, or trusted friend when you are at an impasse.

When making money decisions, be sure you have up-to-date information. Under today's constantly changing laws and regulations, both in banking and old age benefits, we need to keep current. If you do not know your parent's eligibility or entitlements under Social Security, the first step is to visit the local Social Security office. Gather whatever pertinent papers you might need from your parent; assess his assets (home ownership, automobile, savings, insurance, Medicare). Sometimes what a parent thinks he has coming is not correct.

KNOWING WHAT BENEFITS ARE AVAILABLE

Many people confuse Medicare, Medicaid, and Supplemental Security Income. They do not know what is covered in the event of hospitalization or nursing home admittance. Benefits are not automatic; you have to apply. The local Social Security office can give you the information you need. As you gather these facts, you are helping not only your parent, but also yourself—getting a glimpse of what you need to know about your own preparedness for old age.

It is true that in our society the family has undergone gross changes. Since the January 1973 Roe vs. Wade Supreme Court decision for abortion on demand, over 30 million unborn babies have been aborted. Increased divorce and remarriage causes extraordinary family complications; lifestyles include homosexual "families." We are suffering a curse of our own making.

What makes the care and the death of aged parents today (and those not aged) so complicated is the rapid growth of medical technology and availability of life-support systems that not only keep the body alive, but place excessive financial burdens on the patient, the family, and the state. Do not misunderstand that statement! Every patient deserves loving care and the use of medically approved measures to sustain life. But who is to decide who should live and who should die? We are at a dangerous crossroads in our society. Genetic engineering and experimentation, including the use of aborted fetal tissue, provide both threat and promise. Decisions will only be as proper and ethical as those who are in control; therefore, keeping deathbed decisions within the circle of patient, doctor, and family is crucial.

Dr. Henry B. Larzelere, a physician friend, told me:

If you as a doctor are sincere with the family and the patient, the right decision will be made. The atheistic doctors are the ones with the worst problem making a decision. They try to "play God"—try to assume that big role, saying, "I'll have trouble," meaning they worry about themselves. They want laws so they may operate inside a little protective cage. . . . The cake is not baked the same way each time. It must taste good at the end of the baking. That's where faith comes in. If you are not comfortable with the doctor you have selected, get another one!

CHOOSING A DOCTOR

When a parent makes the shift from his own home to yours, or to a nursing home near you, a first concern is to locate the right doctor. In areas where physicians are in short supply, you may have no choice; you may even have a problem finding a doctor or a group practice who will take new patients. Contact the nearest medical school, university teaching hospital, or medical center for names of doctors, stating the age and disability of your parent. You might also consult a floor nurse in a hospital or nursing home or ask friends with elderly parents for suggestions.

If possible choose an older doctor, nearing the time of life himself when he may face geriatric problems. Older doctors are often more interested in those they treat than the treatments they select, more likely to see the whole person, and have a perspective on the ills of the aged person. Don't be afraid to ask questions. How does he feel about various treatments for the dying aged? Is he willing to investigate the basis for a patient's senility? Will he make visits to the nursing home you have selected? If he cannot be reached, who will take the calls? Will he answer specific questions you ask with specific answers? Is he short-tempered or patient with you? Developing communication with him at the beginning makes it easier to deal with him later in the event of your parent's stroke, heart attack, or senile dementia.

WHEN A PARENT LIVES WITH YOU

In Chapter 7, we dealt with some positive ideas for living together, should your solution be having your parent or parents live in your home. I cannot stress enough that firmly but lovingly explaining your family's routines right at the beginning of your new living arrangement, saves more stress. Unless your parent is senile, you must explain the general pattern of life: who works and when, what your children are allowed to do, mealtimes, rules for sharing bathrooms (if necessary); in short, include your parent in the existing pattern of your family's life. Some parents will go out of their way to accommodate you—praise them and thank them!

Others will need to be guided and reminded until the pattern is established.

Sometimes a parent is well enough to assist by baby-sitting and doing light housekeeping and cooking. This can help the families who have two parents who are waged workers.

If your parent has been recently widowed, this traumatic change includes a grieving process. Remember, you cannot replace the husband or wife of your parent; neither can you make up for his or her home, friends, or activities. *You can provide for comfort, but not for happiness.* Insist on privacy for yourself and your spouse, whether or not hurt feelings follow.

Before you decide to have a parent live with you, think it through. Is it the only option financially? Does your spouse approve? Have you previously had a comfortable relationship with this parent? The health of all concerned must be considered under today's intense stress. Remember, your parent is moving into YOUR home, not vice versa. When you also have children at home, this may

149

provoke special problems. Writing about parents in your home, James Halpern PhD, says, "Families can get into trouble when there are coalitions across generational lines. This means that if one spouse consistently takes sides with the grandparent against the other spouse, problems will arise. Similarly, if a grandparent consistently sides with a grandchild against a parent, problems can arise.[2]

THE NURSING HOME

As the ranks of the elderly increase, government, media, churches, and family have focused more on the quality of care in our nursing homes. Once considered a sort of "horror city" and last resort, many (though not all) have been upgraded to provide a competent level of care.

You may want to grade and assess the facilities available to you in the area where you and your parent live.

If your parent has little or no money, check the Department of Social Services (Welfare Department) and the Medicaid or Social Security offices. Some nursing homes are approved for both Medicare and Medicaid, some only for Medicare. Still others will not accept patients who must be admitted on Medicaid funds. Some offer skilled nursing care which means round-the-clock supervision for the severely disabled or ill.

There are facilities which are private or denominational, requiring a down payment for long-term residency; others are public institutions. In looking at the nursing home option, consider three things: finances, level of the parent's disability, future prognosis. A doctor should be involved in your decision. Investigate the nearest nursing homes which offer the care you need and can afford. Private nursing home care can be very expensive, though charges vary greatly.

TAKE A POSITIVE ATTITUDE

As you investigate and pray, ask God to confirm to you His best choice. Look for these ten positive signs as you assess the facilities:

1. The home is clean and neat without appearing sterile and cold.

2. The staff is open and friendly, willing to spend time with you, give you a tour, and answer your questions in full.

3. A general atmosphere of friendliness and caring prevails. Residents' rooms are decorated with mementos from home. Walls are not bare.

4. The staff includes an adequate number of RNs, LPs, and CNAs (Certified Nursing Assistants).

5. The licensed dietician is able to provide special dietary requirements under a doctor's order.

6. Licensed physical therapists are available.

7. Patients are clean, hair combed, and those who are able are up in chairs or wheelchairs by late morning.

8. Check bulletin boards, dayrooms, recreational facilities for programs.

9. Most physicians and families of patients approve the facility.

10. Recent licensure and certification survey results are posted or available.

"In the last few years, federal and state laws have improved the administration of nursing homes," says Elizabeth Kail, who has been an administrator in several homes. "For example, the Omnibus Budget Reconciliation Act of 1990 (OBRA) has revamped the inspection process, with emphasis on the patient or resident rather than just the physical plant. Each patient is individually assessed and/or interviewed for improvement or changes."

151

Other improvements include a mandatory full-time social worker for families (if the facility has 120 or more beds), a director of activities, and fully licensed and certified nursing assistants.

Just because the nursing home is complying with regulations doesn't mean you may be satisfied with the care. However, Dolly Pugh feels that in many homes there's a breakdown of communication. "If you have a complaint," says Dolly, "write it out and request to see the final written complaint. Follow it through. Often communication among the administrator, director of nursing, and charge nurse isn't what it should be."

Dolly is positive, though, about the mandatory interdisciplinary team of staff that meet with the family every three months. "This is a good time to ask questions and see all staff at once."

If you have never visited a nursing home, you may be depressed by patients in wheelchairs and using walkers. Some will be disoriented or withdrawn. If your parent is mentally alert and can hear well, ask if roommates are "paired": those able to relate to one another and enjoy company and activities should be, if possible, in the same room. Extremely ill or senile patients are better paired together. A caring staff will be trained to assess the needs and personalities of patients and attempt to do all they can to make a parent's living situation as pleasant as possible.

Perhaps your parent will spend only a few weeks in the nursing home, returning to his home or yours after a convalescence, but if long-term confinement occurs, you will be entering a new phase of life—one of mixed emotions, a variety of decisions, and wearisome visits. Your obedience to God's Word and the help of the Holy Spirit are vital to you, your parent, and other members of your family.

TIME TO CONSIDER

1. If your parent's physical or mental health is failing, list your options for help and care. (You might want to reread Gwen's experience in chapter 6, "Strength for the Weary").

2. If your parent refuses to move out of his home or receive help, list some options you can try. Is it possible to enlist help from other family members? Why or why not?

3. In what way do your past relationships with parents or siblings affect communication now?

4. Is your parent willing to spend her own money for her care? If not, what are your options? (If there is very little money, get counsel).

5. How can you help your parent face her losses if she feels she is losing control of her life? How can reading scripture together help you both? Find three psalms that can help.

6. If you plan to bring your parent into your home, list the pros and cons first: What will she expect from you and your family? What will you expect from her? Consider space, other family needs, and finances. Talk to others who have parents living with them. Consider holding a family meeting to openly discuss these issues before a final decision is made.

7. How can you assist your parent in her changes and moves and still keep focused on your own priorities? How can you keep focused on the Lord and His help? Read James 4:10 and Isaiah 55: 6-13.

13
...

In Everything
Give Thanks

"Rejoice always; pray without ceasing; in everything give thanks; for this is the will of God in Christ Jesus for you" (I Thess. 5:16-18).

"In everything give thanks?" Marian's hands were raised in a gesture of refusal. "No way can I be thankful for this mess we're in." She went about her duties responsibly, but grimly, caring for a father who was selfish and demanding.

On the other hand, Diane smiled, praised, and thanked the Lord loudly, sweetly telling others how easy it was to be "Mother's helper." At home alone, Diane wept in her pillow, beating her fists in frustration.

I don't think either of these responses is what God intended. None of us *feels* thankful all the time, nor can we be thankful *for* all circumstances, but we can be thankful *in* them. Neither is it right to sound as though all is well and be bitter inside.

Real thanks in all things includes recognizing God's sovereignty, His keeping power, the constant presence of the Holy Spirit. Allowing Him to walk ahead of us, beginning each day by turning it over to Him and, yes, thanking Him daily and consciously, improves our relationship with Him.

Earlier I spoke of the tension of accommodation—the pull between generations and between siblings. Some will be better listeners, more understanding than others. The dark side of life's changes exposes threats, taunts, and reprisals; the light side reveals caring, compromise, and compassion. Sometimes the dark and the light are mixed, causing tension as we determine direction, decisions, and priorities.

RECOGNIZING LOSSES

Both generations suffer losses that must be recognized and acknowledged. Parents, whether accommodating or recalcitrant, often must leave lifelong homes, apartments, prized furniture, cars, friends, churches. Sometimes it means giving over control of finances, schedules, and routines which have been parts of their lives for so long. Depending on the personality and the mental stability of the parent, this presents varying degrees of trauma.

If you are the caregiver, your lifestyle is also affected. Suddenly you have time-consuming tasks that must be integrated with jobs, home duties, and relationships with spouse or children (who are not always in tune with your new responsibility). At this point you must accept what has happened—you can't turn back. You, too, may lose freedoms and time, perhaps space and money as well, in order to care for a parent.

Probably the most devastating loss for you and your

parent is his loss of mental capacity. An examination might uncover depression or other treatable conditions caused by vitamin B deficiency, or hearing and eyesight problems. Sometimes the problem is medication. If your parent has a probable diagnosis of Alzheimer's disease or other dementing illness that cannot be cured, write to Alzheimer's Disease and Related Disorders Association (ADRDA), 360 N. Michigan Ave., Suite 1000, Chicago, IL 60611-1676. Local chapters to help families cope with the stress related to this problem and support groups unite families in similar situations.

ESTABLISHING PRIORITIES

Getting emotionally caught up in the new process of role reversal can cause changes in you and your family that may not surface immediately. In the first stages of moving, while providing new accommodations for your parent (whether in your home or another), you are busy physically and mentally; you are discovering feelings from the past that must be dealt with; you may be enlisting the help of your spouse, children, brothers, or sisters. As events quiet down, you may find that *you* haven't. Your mind stays active at night, you question choices, you overcompensate for your parent's loss by giving too much of your own time.

Subtle changes may then occur. Your husband or wife indicates displeasure or reacts by withdrawal and silence. Other family members may disagree with the choices that were made. It is time, then, to set yourself apart and evaluate your priorities. Remember, all that appears urgent is not necessarily important. If your own life reflects a wholeness from having priorities in order, that wholeness will flow outward, causing others to be calm and purposeful.

How do we accomplish this? First, we must accept life as it is, not as we think it should be.

Wishing it were otherwise is a negative use of energy. Being realistic enables us to list our priorities and goals so that we may integrate them into our lifestyles, as well as to take steps to correct those that are out of order. We must praise and thank God as we work on this. Pray without ceasing (keeping thoughts, needs, and thanks lifted to God). Listen for negative phrases: "I wish. . . ." "I don't like. . . ." "I can't even. . . ." It's impossible. . . ." Consciously practicing positive ways of speaking will help us as well as our listeners.

UNDERSTANDING THE FEELINGS OF OTHERS

Second, wholeness comes from recognizing the needs of others precious to us.

By letting a mother know that we understand her feelings of loss, by praising her for every small acceptance of them, we encourage her to flow with the tide, rather than play tug-of-war with our emotions. She, too, if able, needs to understand our priorities, so honesty is important. If we have a spouse and children at home, their needs must come first.

One conversation with my mother, while she was in the nursing home, shocked me at first but opened the door for me to be honest with her. For some forgotten reason, I needed to skip some visits with her in order to be with my husband, a decision which I shared with my mother.

"I know," she lashed out. "Mothers don't count!"

I realized that, as the eldest of four, my mother had experienced a very close relationship with her own mother. In addition, she was past thirty when she married and had always lived at home. I sat down near her. "Your mother always came first, didn't she?" I asked gently.

"Yes," answered this old lady, now in her late eighties.

"My husband must come first," I told her, and explained that this decision came from God's Word. "You know very well that I love you and care about you. That will always be true."

She calmed down. She did understand. Just as a child, she had felt a temporary disappointment and hurt. I left her room that day feeling whole, because I had not allowed an angry phrase to destroy communication or leave my mother in a state of rejection.

Recognizing the personhood of parents and of spouse and children is not the only route to wholeness. Loving and caring for ourselves, paying attention to our physical needs, our own activities, and rest requirements enables us to be vital, growing persons.

"I had to give up my painting classes," sighed Elizabeth. "Mother expects to see me at the nursing home every day."

Elizabeth had assumed the role of martyr. After her mother died, Elizabeth lost interest in her hobby. She blamed her mother, nurtured an unforgiving heart, and became a disgruntled old lady herself.

Honest and creative thinking can help us continue our own lives in a healthy manner. When Bill and I made our decision to visit the Holy Land, I felt a real peace. Before I left, I made funeral plans for both parents. I selected caskets, talked with the funeral director, picked out clothes, and laid them aside. In the event of a death during our ten-day leave, the body would be held in a closed casket, and the funeral would take place on our return. Some might consider this callous; I believe it was being realistic.

TOUGH LOVE

You cannot change your parent's life situation, his state of health (except by good medical care), his age, or dependency. If he blames you for any of these, refuse to carry this "baggage." Reject this load.

By being reasonably attentive and caring, and doing what is necessary, you exhibit "tough love." Your parent is an imperfect human being who may be carrying baggage from the past that he has never learned to lay down. Why perpetuate this situation by carrying a case full of resentment, too?

Sometimes it is only by looking back that we see ourselves as resentment carriers. We can be so busy acting out our grudges, nursing them, turning them over and over in our minds, allowing them to assail our health, that we are unaware of their devastating effects on us and those they are directed at. Break the chain of resentment and grudges by taking an honest look at them and asking God's forgiveness.

"An important part of family or origin work is resolving our relationship with the people in our families," writes Melody Beattie in her book *Beyond Co-Dependency.*

> This means acknowledging and releasing any intense feelings about family members, so we are free to love and grow. This can mean running the gamut of emotions from denial, hate, rage, disappointment, wishful thinking, resentment, and despair, to acceptance, forgiveness and love. Many adult children wish circumstances and people could have been, or would be different. They weren't and they aren't. And although our feelings toward family members and our childhoods are valid, these feelings can block our growth if we don't resolve them.[1]

Unforgiveness *must* be dealt with. Recognizing that God forgives us when we ask Him is truly a reason for rejoicing; and should bring us to forgive our parents (whether they ask for it or not). The father who left home and rejected you, the mother who told you she never wanted you—yes, you must forgive them if you profess the name of Christ. You need also to share your most precious possession, the love of Jesus, if they do not know Him as Savior.

My mother-in-law once told me that she was the last child, "an unwanted one." She spent her whole life trying to control people, take over situations, prove herself. She didn't know she was crying out, "See me . . . I am important!" No one had ever told her of her importance to God to free her from this shackle.

When my father-in-law died in his sixties, my mother-in-law, a healthy, vital person, "expected" we would come to live with her in her big house. I was then pregnant with my third child. When my husband told her we would not move, she cried out, "What will people think of a son who doesn't want his mother?"

WILL TO FORGIVE

Parents can make us feel guilty, resentful, and unforgiving, but we must will to forgive them and not allow ourselves to be trampled or herded in unhealthy directions.

Later in life, my husband needed his mother's forgiveness for his attitude toward her. She didn't understand why he asked her for it, but she granted it. It was then that a full-blown physical healing occurred in Bill's life. Resentment and lack of forgiveness often block the healing Jesus longs to give.

Guilt complicates life by causing us to do too much or too little for a parent; to overcompensate for a parent's loss or to avoid contact in order to (mistakenly) avoid the sense of guilt. Guilt may cause depression, physical ailments, and loss of energy, which in turn produce hostility as we drag ourselves through the days, trying to perform as good children should. As we feel hostility toward the parent, more guilt results. It is a merry-go-round we don't need to ride. As we *will* to forgive, God will give His grace.

After we lay down the baggage, we experience a freedom that carries us through those last years with a dependent or dying parent. The help of the body of Christ is very crucial for those experiencing these times. If a prayer group, Bible study, fellowship, or prayer partner upholds us at this time, then all—parents, brothers, sisters, and their families—will feel the prayers of God's people.

The time of caring for parents is a difficult one, but it provides an opportunity to exercise our faith, stretch ourselves toward wholeness, become more loving and accepting of others. In turn if we are not called home early, or if the Lord tarries, we too will take our places among the elderly.

As we seek to minister effectively to parents and families, it is well to emphasize a few simple truths to keep ourselves on course: First, spend time daily in prayer and in God's Word. Listen for the guidance of the Holy Spirit. Second, remember that we can provide for our parents' comfort (and it is our duty to do so), but we cannot provide for their happiness. Third, what may seem urgent is not always important. Evaluate choices and action. Fourth, if we need help to free ourselves of unforgiveness, guilt, or resentment, we must seek help from a pastor or other counselor, a trusted friend, or an adult child; get another's perspective on the problem.

Rejoice—for He is Lord! Pray without ceasing—He hears and answers! In everything give thanks for this is God's will in Christ Jesus.

TIME TO CONSIDER

1. This chapter mentions many of the feelings discussed throughout the book: Tension in the family, losses, unforgiveness, guilt, and resentment. Which one is causing you trouble right now? What can you do about it? Be specific.

2. Are you honest about your feelings? How might your past relationship with your parent affect your actions right now?

3. Is it hard for you to be honest with your parent or siblings without being angry? Think of ways to express yourself that could cause others to give a positive response.

4. Both the author and Melody Beattie speak about accepting life the way it is rather than wishing circumstances and people could have been—or would be—different. Why is this so hard for most of us? What does the Bible say about this?

5. What is the difference between giving thanks *for* everything and giving thanks *in* everything? Think of an example from your own life.

6. Meditate on the Virgin Mary's song of praise in Luke 1:46-55. Name the things Mary says God has done. How is God's mercy evident in your life? Write your own song of praise. How does yours differ from Mary's? How are they alike?

Afterword

The One Who Holds My Hand

"The steps of a man are established by the Lord; and He delights in his way. When he falls, he shall not be hurled headlong; because the Lord is the One who holds his hand. I have been young, and now I am old; yet I have not seen the righteous forsaken, or his descendants begging bread. All day long he is gracious and lends; and his descendants are a blessing" (Ps. 37:23-36 NAS).

"Every once in a while," Edith said, "I think, *Oh, I must remember to tell Mother that.* Isn't that crazy—she's been dead for two years."

I have never done that. But those of us whose parents have died have some particular time or place that triggers a pang of remembrance. For me it's when I am selecting a greeting card. I see "To Mother and Dad at Easter," or "To

165

Mother and Dad on Their Anniversary," or "Happy Valentine's Day to My Parents." The first time this occurred, I thought: Never again will I be able to pick out a card for my mother and father.

Soon after Mother's death, my husband looked at me strangely and said, "They're gone—your parents and mine. We're the older generation now."

Whether you are thirty-five or fifty-five, you have probably given some thought—however fleeting—to a picture of yourself as a senior member of your family and community. The earlier you prepare yourself for this in a healthy and constructive manner, the more rewarding that time will be.

Much has been said about "when are we old." However we may reject it, forty (certainly a prime time) is considered the beginning of middle age; and if fifty sounds young and vigorous to you, remember that the American Association of Retired Persons recruits members of that age. Over sixty-five is a phrase used for everything from discussion of retirement to TV commercials selling insurance. Your physiological age (that is, your biological "inner clock") determines when you are a senior citizen.

Whatever our ages, the Lord is the One who holds our hands, and as we pray and seek to do His will, He motivates people and sets in motion help for His people of all generations.

PREPARING FOR OLD AGE

What can we do now, to prepare ourselves for old age as a time of wisdom and fulfillment?

We can

• Spend time with the Lord daily as a discipline and He will guide in plans and decisions.

• Review priorities and goals regularly. Make changes as life changes.

• Stay flexible. Sometimes do something we don't enjoy in order to stay flexible. Deliberately change our schedules and vary our routines often. No ruts allowed.

• Pursue hobbies we like.

• Practice good health rules in the areas of eating, exercise, and rest.

• Refrain from criticizing others, except in context of issues. Allow others freedom to be themselves in Christ.

• Maintain communication with family members, even when we disagree with their opinions or lifestyles. We must listen, be sensitive to their problems, and open to their suggestions. This builds the foundation for cooperation later in life, when we are the elderly parents.

• Practice compassion and kindness.

• Love ourselves in the sense of recognizing our worth in God's sight. Be aware of and do all we can to enhance the good in us.

• Write down the qualities we would like to have when we are old and start now to implement them in our lives.

• Leave our houses in order for those who follow. Prepare now so that our loved ones will not be overwhelmed by our inadequate preparations for death.

As I write, I see the areas in my life that need improvement and renewal. I believe as we examine these suggestions, the Holy Spirit will show us individually where we are negligent and where we can make changes that will give us peace as we age and produce peace in others.

Unfortunately, it is usually true that the older we get, the less accommodating toward others we become. Certainly, we don't want to become dolts or doormats, but we need to understand that each person has his own weaknesses and strengths, his own cares and priorities.

Our imperfections, our failures, our unforgiveness should lead us to seek the Perfect One, to forgive ourselves for failure and forgive others for theirs. The Perfect One is there all the time for the seeking; failure can be put behind us, spurring us on to inspired goals. Forgiveness is not only possible and desirable, it is mandatory if we are to live sanctified lives.

Even before my active commitment to Christ as Lord, and while I was producing and hosting a daily television show, I learned that failure must be put behind me. If a show went badly or I sensed a poor performance, I said to myself, "It's over—there's nothing I can do about it now. Tomorrow I have another chance to do better." Doesn't that translate into our spiritual lives?

The excitement of knowing a faithful God through adversity makes each day worth living. It is matched only by the excitement of sharing the Lord with others—family members, friends, and the people who cross our paths in the course of daily life.

Then we can say with Paul:

I have fought long and hard for my Lord, and through it all I have kept true to him. And now the time has come for me to stop fighting and rest. In heaven a crown is waiting for me which the Lord, the righteous Judge, will give me on that great day of his return. And not just to me, but to all those whose lives show that they are eagerly looking forward to his coming back again (2 Tim. 4:7, 8 TLB).

Source Notes

The appearance of a book title in Aglow's source notes in no way constitutes a recommendation by Women's Aglow Fellowship International or the author. Occasionally an author may refer to or quote from another source as an example or to reinforce a point only.

FOREWORD

1. Administration on Aging fact sheet. (Dept. of Health and Human Services, May, 1993.)

2. AARP Bulletin, June 1992, p. 3.

3. *Aging*, the publication of Health and Human Services, Issue #362, 1991, p. 4.

CHAPTER 3

1. A. J. Russell, editor, *God Calling* (Old Tappan, NJ, Spire Books, Jove Publications for Fleming H. Revell Co. by arrangement with Dodd, Mead & Co., Inc., 1977), p. 100.

2. Henri J. M. Nouwen and Walter Gaffney, *Aging* (Image Books, 1976), p. 113.

3. Jan Otten and Florence D. Shelley, *When Your Parents Grow Old* (New York, Funk & Wagnalls, 1976), pp. 107-108.

CHAPTER 4

1. Pat King, *How Do You Find the Time?* (Lynnwood, WA, Aglow Publications, 1975), p. 101.

2. Dr. Lowell B. Sykes, pastor of Rivermont Presbyterian Church, "Our Comforting God," sermon, preached in Lynchburg, VA, 1982.

3. Ibid.

CHAPTER 5

1. "Study on Improving Mobility and Safety for Older Persons," (special report #218, Washington, D.C., National Research Council, 1988), pp. 38, 39.

2. Donald G. Miller, *The Layman's Bible Commentary*, The Gospel According to Luke, Vol. 18 (Atlanta, GA, John Knox Press, 1959), pp. 118, 119.

CHAPTER 6

1. Emily K. Abel, *Who Cares for the Elderly? Public Policy and the Experience of Adult Daughters* (Philadelphia, Temple University Press, 1991), pp. 57, 58.

2. Barbara Deane, *Caring for Your Aging Parents* (Colorado Springs, CO, NavPress, 1989), p. 74.

CHAPTER 7

1. Dr. Archibald D. Hart, *Feeling Free* (Old Tappan, NJ, Fleming H. Revell, 1979), p. 89.
2. Robert H. Schuller, *Self-Esteem: The New Reformation* (Fort Worth, TX, Word Publishers, 1982), p. 95.

CHAPTER 8

1. Attributed to John Quincy Adams.
2. Maggie Callanan and Patricia Kelley, *Final Gifts* (New York, Poseidon Press, 1992).

CHAPTER 9

1. Church Book for the Evangelical Lutheran Congregation (Philadelphia, Publication Board, 1897), pp. 629-630.
2. Paul Tournier, *Learn to Grow Old* (New York, Harper and Row, 1972), p. 185.
3. Nathan Billig, M.D., *To Be Old and Sad—Understanding Depression in the Elderly* (Lexington, MA, Lexington Books, D.C. Heath and Co., 1987), p. 5.
4. Dr. Archibald D. Hart, *Feeling Free* (Old Tappan, NJ, Fleming H. Revell, 1979), p. 169.

CHAPTER 10

1. Myron Augsburger, *Quench Not the Spirit* (Scottsdale, PA, Herald Press, Choice Books Edition, 1975), p. 57.
2. Catherine Marshall, "The Helper," *Guideposts* (1978), p. 32.
3. Quoted from Dr. R. Maurice Boyd's sermon preached at Centenary United Methodist Church, Lynchburg, VA, May 19, 1992.

CHAPTER 11

1. Paul Ramsey, Ph.D., *Ethics at the Edges of Life* (New Haven, CN, Yale University Press, 1978), p. 156.
2. David Cundiff, M.D., *Euthanasia is not the Answer—a Hospice Physician's View* (Totowa, NJ, Humana Press, 1992), p. 46.
3. C. Everett Koop, M.D., interview in *Lear's* magazine, April, 1992, p. 21.
4. Quote from Allen Jay, M.D., during "NonVoluntary Euthanasia" workshop at the National Right-to-Life Convention, June 11-13, 1992, Washington, D.C.
5. Malcolm Muggeridge. "Human Utopia: The Great Liberal Death Wish," *Christianity Today*, September 3, 1982, p. 42.
6. Paul Ramsay, *Ethics at the Edges of Life* (New Haven, CN, Yale University Press, 1978), p. 187.

CHAPTER 12

1. Barbara Silverstone and Helen Kandel Hyman, *You and Your Aging Parent* (New York, Pantheon Books, 1982), pp. 51, 52.
2. James Halpern, Ph.D., *Helping Your Aging Parents* (New York, McGraw-Hill, 1987), p. 193.

CHAPTER 13

1. Melody Beattie, *Beyond Co-Dependency* (San Francisco, A Harper/Hazelden Book, Harper & Row), p. 87.

Resource List

American Association of Retired Persons (AARP)
1909 K Street NW
Washington, DC 20049
(202) 434-2277

The AARP supplies information and booklets on all subjects related to elder care. A few sample titles: "Miles Away and Still Caring," "Home-Made Money," "Nursing Home Life: A Guide for Residents and Families," "The Right Place at the Right Time: A Guide to Long Term Care Choices," "Handbook about Care in the Home," "Using Your Medicine Wisely: A Guide for the Elderly."

Write for their extensive list at the address above. No charge for AARP members. Annual dues: $8.

Alzheimer's Disease and Related Disorders Association (ADRDA)
919 N. Michigan Ave., Suite 1000
Chicago, IL 60611
1-800-272-3900

Write or call for free basic information packet including where to get more information/aid in your area. National membership in the Alzheimer's Association is $25 which includes newsletters that contain up-to-date information on research, support groups, etc. Your local telephone directory should have your local Alzheimer's Association chapter listed, or consult your city's social services directory.

Administration on Aging
(Department of Health and Human Services)
Office of External Affairs
330 Independence Ave., SW
Washington, DC 20201
(202) 619-1006
(202) 619-3759 FAX

Administration on Aging (AoA) is the advocate agency for older persons and their concerns at the federal level. Write or call for information about its programs, including the Eldercare Volunteer Corps, elders who serve as mentors, tutors, surrogate grandparents, in preschools, schools, after school.

National Association of Area Agencies on Aging (AoA)
Eldercare Locator
600 Maryland Ave., SW
Washington, DC 20024
1-800-677-1116

Older persons, their caregivers, or anyone concerned about the welfare of an older person can contact their Area Agency on Aging for information and referral to services and benefits in their community. (Local agencies are usually listed in the yellow pages under city, or county government headings.) When calling, please provide the older person's address and zip code.

AoA's focus is to help the elderly remain in their own homes as long as possible, by providing information on services such as: home-delivered meals, transportation, legal assistance, housing options, adult day care, senior center programs, home health services, elder abuse prevention programs, and nursing home ombudsman referrals. AoA is a national membership organization of a private, not-for-profit agency with 670 area agencies throughout the U.S.

National Council on Aging
409 Third St., SW
Washington, DC 20024
(202) 479-1200

Provides services to the elderly by furnishing informational resources, and cargiving material. Call or write for a catalog and general informatoin packet (at no charge). National Council on Aging is a professional membership, not-for-profit organization working on several aspects of aging, its issues and services.

American Association of Homes for the Aging
901 E St., NW, Suite 500
Washington, DC 20004-2037
(202) 783-2242

A private, not-for-profit organization that offers a directory of more than 4,000 nursing homes, and continued care (retirement) homes. (***Note:** Though the U.S. government accredits nursing homes, as of this writing, it has not established a standard for accrediting continued care homes.)

National Association of Professional Geriatric Care Managers
655 N Alvernon Way, Suite 108
Tucson, AZ 85711
(602) 881-8008

A private, not-for-profit service that refers requests for caregiving to an agency in caller's local area. Some geriatric care managing services include grocery shopping, house cleaning, practical nursing, other at-home services.

Children of Aging Parents
1609 Woodbourne Rd.
Levittown, PA 19057
(215) 945-6900

Provides information, resources, helps. Send $2.00 and a stamped, self-addressed envelope to Dept. WD for information.

SERVICES AVAILABLE IN MANY COMMUNITIES

Adult daycare centers provide care, activities for up to five days a week. Many are found in neighborhood churches.

Companion aides do not provide medical care, but are available to drop by, help with shopping, letter writing.

Meals On Wheels delivers a hot meal for noontime and a cold meal for supper in one daily trip.

Respite care relieves the caregiver of the responsibility for a family member who needs constant care; provided on a short-term basis either in or out of the home.

Transportation services requires calling ahead to make arrangements. Usually a volunteer effort provided by area agencies on aging.

Visiting nurses come to a person's home and provide medical care such as monitoring blood pressure and medications, and bathing.

AUTHOR'S SUGGESTIONS FOR ADDITIONAL READING

Parent Care
A monthly newsletter for children of aging parents. Contains inspiration from the Bible, encouragement from other caregivers, new product information, tips, responses to readers' questions. Write: Betty Robertson, PO Box 12624, Roanoke, VA 24027-2624. A one-year subscription costs $19.95.

You and Your Aging Parent
Barbara Silverstone and Helen Kandel Hyman
Pantheon Books, (paperback)

The 36-Hour Day; a Family Guide to Caring for Persons with Alzheimer's Disease, Related Dementia Illness and Memory Loss in Later Life
Nancy L. Mace and Peter V. Rabins M.D.
The Johns Hopkins University Press, (paperback)

Caring for Your Aging Parents: When Love is Not Enough
Barbara Deane
NavPress, (paperback)

Compassionate Care

USE THESE PAGES TO NOTE ADDITIONAL REFERENCES, HELPS IN YOUR LOCAL AREA:

Compassionate Care

ADDITIONAL REFERENCES, NOTES

Compassionate Care

ADDITIONAL REFERENCES, NOTES

Compassionate Care

ADDITIONAL REFERENCES, NOTES

Compassionate Care

ADDITIONAL REFERENCES, NOTES

Compassionate Care

A Special Note
to Prospective Aglow Support Group Leaders

In January, 1994, Aglow introduced a new opportunity for existing and prospective Aglow support group leaders. With the publication of our own *Support Group Leader's Guide* by Jennie Newbrough, (Aglow, 1993), came the chance to standardize our training material and award a Certificate of Completion to women who read our leader's guide and successfully complete the worksheets at the back of the book.

Because support group leaders touch some of the most intimate areas of women's lives, new Aglow support group leaders must possess a Certificate of Completion awarded by the Aglow leadership before they can begin leading a group. Those who receive Aglow's Certificate of Completion also must understand that doing so only allows them to lead an Aglow support group within the Aglow ministry.

Jennie Newbrough, Aglow's support group resource person, believes God has been powerfully using these compassionate "safe places" to transform the lives of countless women. If you feel that God is speaking to you about leading a support group around the topic in this book, we urge you to make your desire known to local Aglow leadership. Let's join in sharing Father God's heart for hurting women.

Compassionate Care

Support Groups–
Places of Growth
and Healing

Women are hungry for teaching and nurturing as they grapple with issues that touch them where they live—loss, self-worth, singleness, remarriage, and numerous other felt needs.

God's heart is to heal and restore his people. In fact, Jesus states this clearly in Luke 4:18, 19 when he announces that God has called him to minister to the oppressed, the hurting, and the brokenhearted. We read throughout the entire New Testament how he wants to equip the Body of Christ to join him in reaching out in love and support of the bruised and wounded. Support groups provide this special place where healing can happen—where women are given time and space to be open about themselves in the context of loving acceptance and honest caring.

WHAT IS A SUPPORT GROUP?

• A support group is a small-group setting which offers women a "safe place." The recommended size is from eight to ten people.

• It is a compassionate, nonthreatening, confidential place where women can be open about their struggles and receive caring and support in a biblically-based, Christ-centered atmosphere.

• It is an accepting place, where women are listened to and loved right where they are.

• It is a place where love and truth are shared and the Holy Spirit is present to bring God's healing.

• It is a place where women learn to take responsibility for making Christ-like choices in their own lives.

• A support group has designated leadership. Co-leaders are strongly recommended to share the role of facilitators.

• It is a cohesive and consistent group. This implies "closing" it to additional participants after the second or third meeting before beginning with a new topic.

WHAT SUPPORT GROUPS ARE NOT

• They are not counseling groups.

• They are not places to "fix" or change women.

• They are not Bible study or prayer groups as such, although Scripture and prayer are a natural framework for the meetings.

• They are not places where women concentrate on themselves and "stay there." Instead they provide opportunity to grow in self-responsibility and wholeness in Christ.

Small groups often rotate leadership among participants, but because support groups usually meet for a specific time period with a specific mutual issue, it works well for a team of co-leaders to be responsible for the meetings. As you can see, leadership is important! Let's take a look at it.

WHAT ARE THE PERSONAL LEADERSHIP QUALIFICATIONS OF A SUPPORT GROUP LEADER?

Courage (1 Cor. 16:13, 14)

A leader shows courage in the following ways in her willingness to

• Be open to self-disclosure, admitting her own mistakes and taking the same risks she expects others to take.

• Lovingly explore areas of struggle with women, and look beyond their behavior to hear what's in their hearts.

• Be secure in her own beliefs, sensitive to the Holy Spirit's promptings, and willing to act upon them.

• Draw on her own experiences to help her identify with others in the group and be emotionally touched by them.

• Consistently examine her own life in the light of God's Word and the Holy Spirit's promptings.

• Be direct and honest with members, not use her role to protect herself from interaction with the group.

• Know that wholeness is the goal and that change is a process.

Willingness to Model (Ps. 139:23, 24)

• A group leader should have had moderate victory in her own struggles, with adequate healing having taken place. If she is not whole in the area she is leading, she should at least be fully aware of her unhealed areas and not be defensive of them. She should be open to those who can show her if she is misguiding others by ministering out of her own hurt.

193

Compassionate Care

• She understands that group leaders lead largely by example, by doing what she expects members to do.

• She is no longer "at war" with her past and can be compassionate to those who may have victimized her. Yet she is a "warrior woman," strong in her resistance of Satan with a desire to see other captives set free.

Presence (Gal. 6:2)

• A group leader needs to either have had personal experience with a support group or observed enough so she understands how they function.

• She needs to be emotionally present with the group members, being touched by others' pain, struggles, and joys.

• She needs to be in touch with her own feelings so that she can have compassion for and empathy with the other women.

• She must understand that her role is as a facilitator. She is not to be the answer person nor is she responsible for change in others. Yet she must be able to evidence leadership qualities that enable her to gather a group around her.

Goodwill and Caring (Matt. 22:27, 28)

• A group leader needs to express genuine caring, even for those who are not easy to care for. That takes a commitment to love and a sensitivity to the Holy Spirit.

• She should be able to express caring by (1) inviting women to participate but allowing them to decide how far to go; (2) giving warmth, concern, and support when, and only when, it is genuinely felt; (3) gently confronting a participant when there are obvious discrepancies between her words and her behavior; and (4) encouraging people to be who they are without their masks and shields.

• She will need to be able to maintain focus in the group.

Openness (Eph. 4:15, 16)

• A group leader must be aware of herself, open to others in the group, open to new experiences, and open to lifestyles and values that are different from her own.

• As the leader she needs to have an *attitude* of openness, not revealing every aspect of her personal life, but disclosing enough of herself to give participants a sense of who she is.

• A group leader needs to recognize her own weaknesses and not spend energy concealing them from others. A strong sense of awareness allows her to be vulnerable with the group.

Nondefensiveness (1 Pet. 5:5)

• A group leader needs to be secure in her leadership role. When negative feelings are expressed she must be able to explore them in a nondefensive manner.

Stamina (Eph. 6:10)

• A group leader needs physical and emotional stamina and the ability to withstand pressure and remain vitalized until the group sessions end.

• She must be aware of her own energy level, have outside sources of spiritual and emotional nourishment, and have realistic expectations for the group's progress.

Perspective (Prov. 3:5, 6)

• A group leader needs to cultivate a healthy perspective which allows her to enjoy humor and be comfortable with the release of it at appropriate times in a meeting.

• Although she will hear pain and suffering, she must trust the Lord to do the work and not take responsibility for what he alone can do.

• She needs to have a good sense of our human condition

and God's love, as well as a good sense of timing that allows her to trust the Holy Spirit to work in the women's lives.

Creativity (Phil. 1:9-11)

• She needs to be flexible and spontaneous, able to discover fresh ways to approach each session.

WHAT SPECIFIC SKILLS DOES A LEADER NEED?

A support group leader needs to be competent and comfortable with basic group communications skills. The following five are essential for healthy and open interaction:

Rephrase

• Paraphrase back to the speaker what you thought she said. Example: "I hear you saying that you felt. . . ."

Clarify

• To make sure you heard correctly, ask the speaker to explain further. Example: "I'm not hearing exactly what you meant when you said. . . ."

Extend

• Encourage the speaker to be more specific. Example: "Can you give us an example. . . ."

Ask for Input

• Give the other women opportunity to share their opinions. Example: "Does anyone else have any insight on this?"

Be Personal and Specific

• Use women's names and convey "I" messages instead of "you" messages. "I'm feeling afraid of your reaction, " instead of "You scare me."

ADDITIONAL COMMUNICATION SKILLS

Active Listening

• A good listener learns to "hear" more than the words that are spoken. She absorbs the content, notes the gestures, the body language, the subtle changes in voice or expression, and senses the unspoken underlying messages.

• As a good listener, a leader will need to discern those in the group who need professional counseling and be willing to address this.

Empathy

• This requires sensing the subjective world of the participant—and caring. Of grasping another's experience and at the same time listening objectively.

Respect and Positive Regard

• In giving support, leaders need to draw on the positive assets of the members. Where differences occur, there needs to be open and honest appreciation and acceptance.

• Leaders must be able to maintain confidentiality and instill that emphasis in the group.

Expressing Warmth

• Smiling is especially important in communicating warmth to a group. Other nonverbal expressions are voice tone, posture, body language, and facial expression.

Genuineness

• Leaders need to be real, to be themselves in relating with others, to be authentic and spontaneous, to realize that the Holy Spirit works naturally.

WHAT DOES A LEADER ACTUALLY DO?

The leader will need to establish the atmosphere of the support group and show by her style how to relate lovingly and helpfully in the group. She needs to have God's heart for God's people. The following is an outline of specific tasks.

She organizes logistics

• The leader helps arrange initial details of the early meetings—time, place, books, etc.

She provides a sense of purpose and vision

• She reminds the group of their purpose from time to time so that the group remains focused. (Note: Leaders need to be aware that much secular material, though good in information, is humanistic in application. "I" and "self" are the primary focus, rather than Christ.)

She acts as the initiator

• She makes sure everyone knows each other, helps them get acquainted and feel comfortable with each other. Makes sure meetings start and end on time.

She continues as an encourager to group members

• This basically means encouraging feelings to be expressed, keeping the atmosphere nonjudgmental and accepting, giving feedback, answering questions, clarifying things that were expressed, etc. Praying with and for members.

She sets expectations

• She models openness and interest in the group. She must be willing to take risks by resolving conflicts and clarifying intentions. She holds up standards of confidentiality personally and by reminding the group at each meeting. Confidentiality is crucial to the health of a group, and women should not divulge any private sharing, even to spouses, family, etc.

• She must be watchful and able to guide individuals away from destructive responses. Example: "I have a right to be hurt." She will need to always separate the person from her behavior, meeting the person where she is. Example: "We accept that you are hurt. Do you need to talk about it?"

She is sensitive to the Spirit

• She must know when someone needs to be referred to a professional counselor, pastor, etc., and be willing to work that problem through.

• She should be comfortable in ministering freely in the gifts of the Holy Spirit.

She gives the guidelines

• It is important that the women know the "ground rules." The leader needs to repeat these often and *always* when newcomers attend. The following are basic support group guidelines:

1. You have come to give and receive support. No "fixing." We are to listen, support, and be supported by one another, not give advice.

2. Let other members talk. Please let them finish without interruption.

3. Try to step over any fear of sharing in the group. Yet do not monopolize the group's time.

4. Be interested in what someone else shares. Listen with your heart. Never converse privately with someone while another woman is talking or belittle her beliefs or expressions.

5. Be committed to express your feelings from the heart. Encourage others to do the same. It's all right to feel angry, to laugh, or to cry.

6. Help others own their feelings and take responsibility for change in their lives. Don't jump in with an easy answer or a story on how you conquered their problem or automatically give scripture as a "pat answer." Relate to where they are.

7. Avoid accusing or blaming. Speak in the "I" mode about how something or someone made you feel. Example: "I felt angry when. . . ."

8. Avoid ill-timed humor to lighten emotionally charged times. Let participants work through their sharing even if it is hard.

9. Keep names and sharing of other group members confidential.

10. Because we are all in various stages of growth, please give others permission to be where they are in their growth. This is a "safe place" for all to grow and share their lives.

She handles group discussion

Everyone is different. Your support group will have a variety of personalities. As a leader you will need to protect the group from problem behavior and help the individuals work through it. The following are examples of ways to help each person contribute so that the group benefits:

THEIR BEHAVIOR	YOUR ACTION
Too talkative	Interject by summarizing what the talker is saying. Turn to someone else in the group and redirect a question: "Elaine, what do you feel about that?"

A "fixer"	Show appreciation for their help and insight. Then direct a question to someone else. It is important to draw others in so that the woman needing help gets a healthy perspective on her situation and doesn't close off with a quickie solution.
Rambler	Thank them. If necessary, even break in, comment briefly, and move the discussion on.
Antagonist	Recognize legitimate objections when you can. Turn their comments to a constructive view. If all else fails, discuss the attitude privately and ask for their help.
Obstinate	Ask them to clarify. They may honestly not understand what you're talking about. Enlist others to help them see the point. If that doesn't work, tell them you will discuss the matter after the meeting.
Wrong topic	Focus on the subject. Say something such as: "Mary, that's interesting, but tonight we're talking about. . . ."
Her own problem	Bring it into the discussion if it is related. Otherwise, acknowledge

201

the problem and say: "Yes, I can see why that hurts you. Could we talk about it privately?"

Controversial questions	State clearly what you can or cannot discuss. Say something such as: "Problems do exist, but we do not discuss political issues here."
Side conversations	Stop and draw them into your discussion by asking for their ideas.
Personality clash	If a dispute erupts, cut across with a direct question on the topic. Bring others into the discussion: "Let's concentrate on the issue and not make this a personal thing."
Wrong choice of words	Point out that their idea is good and then help them by putting their idea into your words. Protect them from ridicule.
Definitely wrong	Make a clear comment, in an affirming way. "That's another point of view and of course you're entitled to your opinion." Then move on.
Bored	Try to find where their area of interest is. Draw them in to share their experience.

Question you can't answer	Redirect the question to the group. If you don't know the answer, say so and offer to find out.
Never participates	Use direct questions. Remind the group that they will get more out of the meeting when they open up.
Quiet, unsure of self	Affirm them in the eyes of the group. Ask direct questions you are sure they can answer.

She evaluates the meeting

• Support groups are a growing experience for everyone, including the leader. Don't be afraid to deal with habitual problems.

• Periodically involve the total group in evaluating how things are going.

She understands conflict and can handle it positively

• She understands the biblical pattern for making peace with our sisters in Christ. (See Matthew 5:9 and Romans 14:19.)

• She understands that Jesus has given us clear guidelines to resolve conflict and effect reconciliation and that our motive must be to demonstrate God's love, not vengeance. (See Matthew 5:23, 24 and Matthew 18:15-17.)

• She understands that we approach all situations humbly, knowing that none of us is without sin (Gal. 6:1-4) and that we are seeking reconciliation and forgiveness, not proving who is right and who is wrong.

• She avoids sermonizing.

• She knows that every group will experience conflict

on their way to becoming mature and effective, but uses it to help clarify goals and boundaries for the group.

• She defines and describes the conflict as "our group problem."

• She deals with issues rather than personalities.

• She takes one issue at a time.

• She tries to catch issues while they are small rather than letting them escalate over time.

• She invites cooperation, rather than intimidating or giving ultimatums.

• She expresses need for full disclosure of all the facts rather than allowing hidden agendas or leftover hurt feelings.

• She tries to maintain a friendly, trusting attitude.

• She recognizes others' feelings and concerns and opts for a "win-win" feeling rather than an "us and them" attitude.

• She encourages the expression of as many new ideas and as much new information as possible to broaden the perspective of all involved.

• She involves every woman in the conflict at a common meeting.

• She clarifies whether she is dealing with one conflict or several on-going ones.

She knows how to use feedback

• Feedback helps another person get information on her behavior.

• Feedback is essential in a support group to help the women keep on target and more effectively move through her problems.

• She helps make feedback specific. Example: "Just now when we were talking about forgiveness, you changed the subject and started to blame your brother."

- She directs feedback toward behavior that the receiver can do something about. Example: "Would you like to make a choice to release your judgment against your friend?"

- She takes into account the needs of both the receiver and the giver of feedback. It can be destructive if it's given to "straighten out" someone, rather than lovingly point out where that person is.

- She knows feedback is most useful when it is asked for. She can say: "Margaret, are you open to some feedback?"

- She watches for good timing. She tries to give feedback at the earliest opportunity after the given behavior occurs.

- She checks to ensure clear communication. One way of doing this is to have the receiver paraphrase the feedback to see if that is what the sender meant. Example: "I heard you saying that I need to examine my motives for. . . ."

ONE FINAL WORD

Be encouraged if the Lord has called you to be a support group leader or a member of a group. The Lord promises to do the work of healing, to be with us, to grant us patience, love, mercy—everything we need to follow His commission to love. There will be hard and even painful times. But we can count on Him. "He who began a good work in you (in us) will carry it on to completion until the day of Christ Jesus" (Phil. 1:6).

BOOKS BY AGLOW PUBLICATIONS

Heart Issues

Stanley Baldwin   **If I'm Created in God's Image Why Does It Hurt to Look in the Mirror?**
A True View of You

Janet Bly   **Friends Forever**
The Art of Lifetime Relationships

Michelle Cresse   **Beyond Fear**
The Quantum Leap to Courageous Living

Jigsaw Families
Solving the Puzzle of Remarriage

Marilyn Fanning   **Compassionate Care**
Practical Love for Your Aging Parents

Denise George   A Longing Heart Hears
God's Gentle Whisper

Heather Harpham   **Daddy, Where Were You?**
Healing for the Father-deprived Daughter

Diana Kruger   **Who Says Winners Never Lose?**
Profiting from Life's Painful Detours

Pam Ravan	**Sock Hunting and Other Pursuits of the Working Mother**
Patricia Rushford	**Lost in the Money Maze?** How to Find Your Way Through
Marie Sontag	**When Love is Not Perfect** Discover God's Re-parenting Process

General Books

Barbara Cook	**Love and Its Counterfeits**
Marion Duckworth	**What's Real Anyway?** Eternal Living in an Everyday World
Irene Endicott	**Grandparenting Redefined** Guidance for Today's Changing Family
Jane Hansen with Carol Greenwood	**Inside a Woman** Revealing Her Longings, Pain, and the Journey to Love
Ranelda Mack Hunsicker	**Secrets** Unlocking the Mystery of Intimacy With God
Kathy Collard Miller	**Sure Footing in a Shaky World** A Woman's Journey to Security

Jennie Newbrough	**Support Group Leader's Guide**
Quin Sherrer	**How to Pray for Your Children**
Quin Sherrer with Ruthanne Garlock	**How to Forgive Your Children**
Joanne Smith and Judy Biggs	**How to Say Goodbye** Working through Personal Grief

We at Aglow encourage you to stop in at your Christian bookstore and pick up these books. If you do not have access to a Christian bookstore, you may order toll free at 1-800-755-2456.

Inquiries regarding speaking availability and other correspondence may be directed to Marilyn Fanning at the following address:

Marilyn Fanning
1129 Rugby Road
Lynchburg, VA 24503